AS ABOVE

SO BELOW

THE QUANTUM TEACHINGS OF JESUS

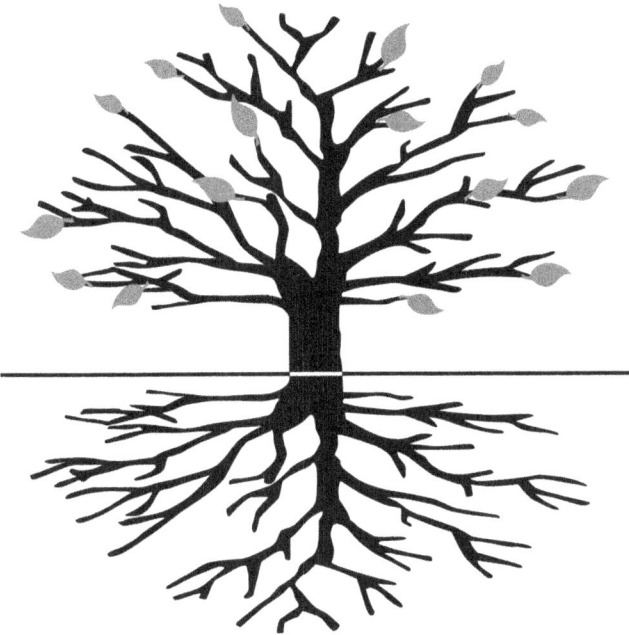

ERIC STEVEN RANKIN

Written by Eric Steven Rankin

Cover by Colleen Hennes Riemer

Chrome Skies Photography & Design

chromeskies.com

Publication Design by Lesley Wexler

ahaincdesign.com

ISBN 979-8-218-15628-2

DEDICATION

This book is dedicated to all spiritual seekers.

Love, honor, and forgiveness are not exclusive to any one religion or belief system, and it is my hope that the words written in these pages serve as a reminder that we are all an expression of the divine remembering our way home.

Contents

Acknowledgements

Over the course of years, many dear friends have
offered invaluable inspiration and guidance,
while others have volunteered their expertise and
knowledge in the realms of science, religious history
and philosophy. To everyone who has so generously
gifted their time, energy, and support for this project,
I am grateful to you beyond measure.

Prologue

I imagine there are many people who, like me, grew up with some denomination of Christianity playing a significant role in their formative years, only to feel its impact fade later in life.

I was born into what I would now call a moderately Christian household in the early 1960s. We said grace at meals, prayed at bedtime, and attended church on a semi-regular basis. And though we were all comfortable performing these rituals, conversations about what any of us actually believed regarding Jesus were rare. My dad, a respected bank manager, had his opinions concerning God and the Christian faith, but he kept them mostly to himself. My mother had a much deeper backstory concerning her religious upbringing, yet she also was not one to share much about it with others. She was raised as a Jehovah's Witness, but eventually excused herself from its strict doctrines and evangelical demands to become what she considered to be a more traditional wife and mother.

During my childhood years, we attended a few different churches before finally being drawn to Seventh Day Adventism, where the only downside I experienced was that services were held on Saturday mornings, right when all the new cartoons were on TV!

Soon after, I was enrolled in an Adventist academy, but once I hit my teens, I was back in public school and pretty much set free to explore how much or little influence Jesus would have on the rest of my life.

From my college years to the present moment, I have been a curious and often skeptical spiritual seeker. I have studied and, at times, followed the principles of different belief systems; from Daoism and Buddhism to various "New Thought" ideologies. All the while, certain aspects of my Christian upbringing continued to percolate in the back of my mind, and every so often I found myself rereading parts of the Bible. I must admit, however, that doing so often reminded me why its teachings had become less relevant to my life. The Old Testament, with its patriarchal stories full of fear, violence, and a jealous God ruling over a sinful world held little appeal. Neither did most of the New Testament, which was heavily influenced by a man known as Paul the Apostle, a Jewish convert who some historians believe was less concerned with sharing the actual teachings of Jesus than being the founder of a powerful new religion and church.

With the majority of the Bible no longer resonating with me, the only writings that still had any lasting allure were the Gospels. These are the four short Books of Matthew, Mark, Luke and John, each which recounts the life and ministry of a man named Yeshua, who lived in the tumultuous times of Roman occupation of Israel roughly 2,000 years ago.

The word *Gospel* means "Good News," a term which aptly sums up the primary message of Jesus' ministry—that there is an intelligent and loving Source of Creation who cares for all things in the universe, including you and me. Jesus took it as his mission to share this good news with everyone who crossed his path, and this was the Jesus I could sympathize with; a rebel pacifist whose ministry was based on compassion, service, forgiveness and love.

Yet my questioning mind, now armed with knowledge gleaned from other religions, resisted some things about the canonized Gospels. First, there was the issue of how they were chosen to be included in the Bible, while other narratives written about Jesus were not. It's far too long of a story to recount here, but it's worth mentioning that there are indeed other Gospels; most notably of Mary, Thomas, Philip and Judas. Many people have never read or even heard of these other stories concerning Jesus, yet these books seem important to the process of fleshing out a more complete picture of who he was and how he lived.

Also, though I was taught early on that every word in the Bible was a statement of fact, I became aware that conflicting details regarding certain events can be found within its pages. For instance, there are two distinctly different accounts concerning Jesus' betrayer, Judas Iscariot. The story all Christians have heard is that he accepted 30 pieces of silver from Jewish priests to reveal Jesus' whereabouts, then returned the money before hanging himself in a field. But in the Book of Acts, it is reported that Judas kept the money and used it to buy a plot of land before falling in a ditch and dying there. I grew up believing in the infallibility of the Bible, so to read such conflicting accounts was unsettling. What other inaccuracies might there be?

This question inspired me to dig deeper as to where, when, and by whom the Gospels were written. As most biblical scholars now believe, the first known Gospel, which was most likely the Book of Mark, was authored no less than 60 years following Jesus' death. Growing up, I had always imagined his disciples feverishly taking note of every word he spoke, but this is not the case. Instead, we have a decades-long span of time where people shared oral versions of the birth, life, ministry and death of Jesus before a single word was ever written about him. And when they were finally transcribed, they were not penned in the Aramaic language Jesus spoke, but in an ancient form of Greek.

It is not hard to imagine that some of Jesus' nuanced teachings could have been misquoted in the process of translation from Aramaic to Greek to Latin to every modern-day language. What's more, as any police officer will tell you, it is almost impossible to interview multiple witnesses of an accident or crime and get a corroborative account of what happened. Multiply this process by thousands of people over the span of decades and you begin to see how challenging it is to fact-check the origins of one of the largest and most influential religions on Earth.

This isn't to say that the Gospels are fabrications. It's just that there may be some parts in them that were either interpreted incorrectly, or intentionally altered to align with a growing evangelical movement already set in motion by the apostle Paul.

For instance, if you read all four of these canonized books, what becomes clear is that Jesus' ministry was mostly concerned with the importance of a person's thoughts, words and conduct. By overwhelming majority, his teachings were calls to action rather than worship, yet over time his message has been inverted to worshipping him as a personal savior more than taking responsibility for one's own behavior. Did he really suggest that people should bow before him because of his intimate relationship with God, or was he asking them to emulate his lifestyle as a way to know God more intimately? This is a question each of us must ask as we consider the process of placing our faith in someone who lived 2,000 years ago and was not quoted in writing for over a half century following his death.

To give an example, take the familiar passage in the Book of John, where Jesus says, "I am the way, the truth and the life." These certainly sound like the words of someone demanding to be revered. But what if, through years of retellings and numerous translations, this quote became skewed so that it no longer conveyed its original meaning? To me, this passage feels much more aligned with the rest of his teachings if it is expressed as, *"The way I am* is the way, the truth and the life," a minor edit which instantly takes the impetus off of worship and invites us to emulate his actions.

Eventually, an idea began to creep into my consciousness. I imagined my favorite Gospel, the Book of Matthew, interpreted in a way that resonates with modern discoveries made in the fields of comparative religion, Eastern philosophy, archeology, and, especially, quantum physics.

As the study of physics continues to advance, scientists are amazed at the strange and often unpredictable nature of reality. Einstein was one of the first physicists to recognize that the momentous discoveries made by Isaac Newton in the 1600s were just the tip of the iceberg concerning the laws of energy, motion, light and gravity. Today, it is common knowledge in the scientific community that there is no such thing as "matter," that gravity can warp space and time, that an observer can affect the outcome of an experiment, and that subatomic particles are mysteriously entangled to create one giant organism we call the universe.

The curious thing is, many of Jesus' teachings coincide with what we now know about how the mechanics of life work on a quantum level. Suddenly, his words concerning the Kingdom of Heaven, prayer, and the power of belief sound incredibly similar to modern notions of parallel realities, resonance, and the laws of cause and effect. In a telling passage from the Gospel of Thomas, Jesus' disciples ask how they are to explain to others that the very essence of God resides within him. To this he answers, "Tell them that I am motion and rest," which seems to reveal his awareness that pulse, frequency, and vibration are the fundamental forces behind all creation, the same conclusion Nikola Tesla made nearly twenty centuries later.

This book—a reimagined Gospel of Matthew featuring personal reflections following each chapter—is the product of my curiosity and research. To be as transparent as possible, I wrote much of it over 25 years ago, then shelved it before sending it to any agents or publishers. At the time, I remember wondering who would want to read it, as it was probably going to seem blasphemous to most Christians or too religious to everyone else.

But now, I have come to realize that there may be space for such a project. Rather than being inflammatory, I see it as a tool that may help bridge the gap separating science and spirit.

I do want to address two troubling issues I had during the process of transcribing this book. Firstly, as was common in the day, there is a strong patriarchal overtone not only in the Gospels, but to the entire Bible. Jesus refers to what we now relate to as God, Source, Spirit, First Cause or the Divine in the masculine form only. In other words, God is always expressed as "He" and I did not bother trying to address every mention of "Him" with any other pronoun. Similarly, when Jesus teaches, he usually mentions "man" or "mankind" to mean all of humanity. This is a common practice even to this day, and it is my hope that you can read this book without being offended by the ubiquitous male pronouns that have permeated religious texts and world literature since the dawn of written history.

Secondly, though Jesus was a practicing Jew his entire life, he was obviously dismayed and agitated by the conduct of certain Jewish priests and scholars. I must admit that there were times when I winced at some of his harsh and accusatory words concerning these high-ranking officials, but I'm quite sure he would have been similarly critical of the leaders of many other organized religions. To the point, I believe he was saying that any dogmatic practice or expression of spiritual elitism is counterproductive to the process of learning more about who and what God truly is.

This book has served a cathartic purpose in my life, and it is my hope that you will read it with the same curious mind and open heart I employed while writing it.

CHAPTER ONE

A Miraculous Beginning

Jesus of Nazareth was born into a family that could trace its lineage back forty-two generations to Abraham, the founding father of the Jewish religion.

As the story goes, a young woman named Mary was engaged to a humble carpenter named Joseph. Though they had never had sexual intercourse, Joseph found out that Mary was pregnant. A noble and compassionate man, Joseph wondered how they would handle this development without being disgraced by their community.

During a dream, Joseph was told by an angel that the baby in Mary's womb was conceived in a supernatural way, and that he should continue with his plans to marry her. In the dream, the angel instructed Joseph to name the baby Jesus, which means "*God Saves*," because the child would demonstrate like no human before him the gift of God's grace and forgiveness.

These events seem to confirm a mysterious Jewish prophecy stating that a virgin shall bear a son whose name will mean, "*God is with us.*"

Joseph awoke and decided to do exactly as the angel in the dream had instructed.

Reflections

I love a good mystery, and for many years the canonized Gospels have inspired me to put on my detective hat and examine the evidence concerning one of the greatest spiritual mysteries ever told.

After reading different research papers concerning the origins of the Gospels, I began to wonder who, in fact, wrote the Book of Matthew. At first, it seemed almost sacrilegious to consider it had been created by anyone other than Jesus' disciple of the same name, but years of investigation have revealed some discrepancies.

Firstly, as most Bible historians now agree, *none* of the Gospels in the New Testament are the product of any of Jesus' disciples or apostles. We are so comfortable seeing the names of Matthew, Mark, Luke and John at the beginning of each book that this scholarly consensus is not only confounding, it also opens the door to speculation as to when and by whom these works were originally drafted. At present, most experts on the subject concur that the apostles' names were attached somewhere between 50 to 100 years after their anonymous authorship.

Secondly, even if we do accept the idea that Matthew wrote this particular Gospel, we face other challenges. For instance, at no time does he ever refer to himself in the first person, as in, "*I* saw Jesus perform miracles, or *I* felt compelled to follow him."

The last and, in my view, most daunting obstacle is the writer's perspective, which in literature is known as "the omniscient narrator." This describes an author who, while telling a story, reveals things he or she could not possibly know. For example, Matthew's description of Jesus' miraculous birth, baptism and even resurrection could not possibly be his own account, as he was not there to witness any of these moments first-hand.

My personal supposition is that, before a single word was ever written about him, oral legends concerning Jesus grew more miraculous with each retelling over time, as is the case with other legendary figures. For instance, the Buddha was supposedly conceived by a heavenly white elephant and human mother, then later delivered painlessly through her side by the deities Brahma and Indra. Later in history, Romulus, the founder and first king of Rome, was said to have been born to an earthly mother and Mars, the God of War, then nursed and raised with his twin brother by a female wolf. More recently, Alexander the Great was reportedly fathered by Zeus, the most powerful god in ancient Greece.

Do fantastical accounts like these make the profound teachings of Jesus less significant? For me, they do not. Rather, they simply reveal that historians and storytellers often overstate actual events to make them more memorable. This is why, when I read the gospels, I focus more on the words attributed to Jesus himself than the grandiose details of his life that may have been embellished by others. In the end, Jesus' words are what matter most, and they are as powerful now as when they were first spoken over 2,000 years ago.

CHAPTER TWO

Proclamation and Danger

Jesus was born in Bethlehem, a small village in the territory of Judah, during Rome's occupation of Israel. It is said that around this time a few wise astrologers, led by a particular star in the eastern sky, arrived into town asking about a newborn king of the Jews. "We're on a pilgrimage to worship him," they said.

Upon hearing this, Herod, the Roman king of Judea, became concerned about a potential challenge to his power and legitimacy. He asked the local priests about ancient Jewish prophecies stating that a Messiah would one day come and vanquish every enemy of their faith. When the priests replied that this mighty savior would be born in Bethlehem, Herod considered this a very real threat both to himself and Roman rule of the land. Under false pretense, Herod got the astrologers to agree to search for the child and report back on his whereabouts.

No one knows how long they searched, but eventually they came upon the dwelling where Jesus lived. With humility and reverence, they entered to find the child cradled in his mother's arms. Bowing before this newborn king, they presented him with valuable gifts, which they had brought with them on their journey.

But in a vision later that night, the astrologers were warned not to report back to Herod and to leave for their homeland immediately.

Meanwhile, Joseph received a prophetic vision of his own. He was made aware that Herod was on the hunt for Jesus and that he should flee with his family to Egypt until further notice. Joseph complied and lived there with his family until Herod died. These events fulfilled another ancient Jewish prophecy which said, "*I called my son out of Egypt.*"

Not knowing that Jesus had already been whisked away to safety, Herod ordered the death of every boy two-years-old and younger who lived in the area. There was an ancient prophecy of Rachel lamenting the death of her children, which may have been referring to this ruling made by Herod.

During one last visitation, Joseph was informed that Herod was dead and that it was safe to return to Israel. Joseph at first headed back to Bethlehem with his family, but was concerned that Herod's son would search out Jesus with the same vengeance.

With this in mind, Joseph decided to move his family to a little village called Nazareth, which is in the region of Galilee. There is another old prophecy which stated, "*He shall be called a Nazarene.*"

Reflections

The story of Jesus' birth and visitation by "three wise men" is widely known and, of course, replicated in nativity scenes all over the world at Christmas time. I have no idea how the Gospel of

Matthew's plural use of *magi* (magician or astrologer), became specifically three over the course of centuries, but there are more important issues to consider in this narrative.

Biblical historians often look for corroborating information in documents of the same era to flesh out the truth regarding certain passages in the Bible. And while this sometimes works in their favor, at other times it does not. For instance, Roman documentarians were known for their careful recording of significant edicts and mandates of the day, yet nowhere do they mention Herod's order to kill all boys two-years-old or younger in the region of Bethlehem. Had this order been given, official Jewish scribes would have certainly recorded this horrific event, yet no such records exist.

What most scholars now believe is that, to give this narrative a certain sense of drama and appeal to Jewish culture, it was most certainly inspired from the story of Moses, the infant son of Israelite slaves living in Egypt roughly two thousand years earlier. As passages from the Old Testament Book of Exodus explain, when the Pharaoh Ramses became aware that a Jewish infant would one day threaten his reign over the Israelites, he ordered the massacre of every first-born Israeli child in the region. Today, we know that many biblical stories—including those of Adam and Eve, Noah and the ark, even a "divine son" who is resurrected after three days—were actually inspired by much older legends, many written thousands of years earlier by ancient Sumerians.

These "borrowed" narratives can lead us to question the validity of certain historical facts, which may either support or renounce certain biblical stories. But as I think about Jesus and the significant role he has played in humanity's spiritual evolution, I find myself relying less on scant historical details and more on the broader messages conveyed through his conduct and teachings.

CHAPTER THREE

The Dawn of a New Era

While Jesus was growing up in Nazareth, an interesting preacher known as John the Baptist had set up camp along the banks of the Jordan River. As Jews traditionally did not baptize people, John was letting it be known that, rather than adhering to the dogmatic laws and rules of a specific religion, he immersed people in the river to symbolize the cleansing gift of redemption that God offers everyone. He said things like, "Purify yourselves from the inside-out and you can experience the Kingdom of Heaven right here and now!" There was a prophecy by Isaiah that said, *"A thunder in the desert will announce God's arrival,"* which may refer to John.

John was a unique individual in every respect. Rather than fine clothes, he wore a thick coat made of camel hair, which was held together with a simple leather strap. And instead of eating rich food, he lived on locusts and wild honey. Even so, people came from miles away to hear his words, with many of them accepting the invitation to turn their sinful lives around by being baptized in the Jordan.

Eventually, even the strictest adherents to the laws of Judaism came down to be baptized, which did not settle well with John. "You brood of snakes!" he yelled. "What are you doing here? Do you think a simple dunking in a river is going to make some kind of miraculous difference in your life? What this baptism represents is a complete restructuring of your soul from the inside out! And don't think that, just because Abraham is an ancestor of yours, you've got any special favor with your Heavenly Father. What counts is how you're living your life right now. Are you a tree growing in true spiritual awareness, or are you dead wood ready for the fire? The decision is yours.

"Let me tell you something: I've been here doing these baptisms for a while now, trying to get you to look within yourselves for the true Kingdom of Heaven, but there is someone coming who will do this on a level I can't even imagine. He will spell out for you exactly how to clean house in your souls so that the very essence of Spirit will have a place to reside within you."

Eventually, Jesus, now a man of around thirty years old, showed up at the river asking John to baptize him.

Realizing that Jesus was the special person he had been telling others about, John bowed down and said, "Master, it is you who should be baptizing me!"

But Jesus insisted that this was the way it should be. "My ministry, which begins today with this baptism, is to shed light on centuries of darkness."

With great humility, John did as he was instructed and baptized Jesus.

Cradled in John's arms, Jesus arose from the river realizing he had been transformed by the experience. In the deepest state of holiness and adoration, he felt the essence of God descend upon him like a dove.

Suddenly, the clouds overhead departed, and a voice from above could be heard saying, "This is My son, who I love. With this man I am well pleased."

In that moment, Jesus came to realize that he was one with the very Source of Creation, and the Source of Creation was one with him.

Reflections

As you have probably noticed, many years have passed since the prior chapter, and we realize that Jesus is now a grown man. While his exact age is not known at this point in the story, most scholars believe he is in his early thirties when he comes to be baptized in the Jordan River.

What was he doing from the time he was a young boy until the moment he met John the Baptist? No one knows for sure, but there are many theories. Some people believe he traveled widely throughout the region and gleaned spiritual knowledge from other Mediterranean cultures. Others think he somehow became exposed to Far-Eastern teachings like Buddhism, which predates Christianity by roughly 500 years. These may be rather far-reaching suppositions, but one thing we do know is that both Jesus and John the Baptist held unique spiritual ideas and were non-conformists in the Jewish tradition. This becomes immediately apparent when we consider John's role and title, as traditional Jews do not practice the ritual of baptism.

It is quite possible that both men were loose adherents to the outlying sect of the Judaic Essenes, desert nomads who lived a life of poverty and service, but even this is conjecture. One thing which does become clear is that John was delivering a very unique message; letting everyone know that the Kingdom of Heaven is not some place you go to after you die, but a state of being one can experience in every moment right here on Earth. Expressing this sentiment in the presence of Jewish priests and scholars must have been incendiary, as the proclamation that people could commune and live in God's grace without the need of holy intermediaries opposed Jewish religion and social traditions of the time.

It is such a beautiful and profound moment when Jesus emerges from the water, for this is when he has the epiphany that he is one with everything, and everything—including God—is one with him.

Environmentalist John Muir arrived at this same conclusion when, looking out over the meadows, streams, trees and massive granite cliffs of Yosemite, he said, "When we try to pick out anything by itself, we find it hitched to everything else in the universe." This realization, which can truly be considered a rapturous experience, comes in different ways to different people, whether it's Albert Einstein, St. Francis of Assisi, the Buddha, or a humble carpenter's son named Yeshua.

Chapter Four

A Test of Faith

Jesus, after accepting his spiritual anointing, knew there could only be one way to prove to himself that he had fully embraced the gift of God's grace. He had to face his personal demons of fear, doubt, judgment and pride. He prepared for this test of character by heading out into the wilderness, praying and fasting for many days.

As could be expected, before long the voice of temptation presented itself, saying, "Now that you fully understand how you are an intrinsic part of all creation, you know that you could turn these stones into bread and eat if you wanted to!"

But Spirit's true voice within him responded, "Maybe so, but that bread would only nourish my physical body, which is nowhere near as important as my spiritual body. No, I would be far better off dying with my eternal soul pure and intact than surviving another day here on Earth unable to resist temptations of the flesh."

For his second test, the inner voice of fear and doubt led him to the Holy City and directed him to sit high atop a temple. "Since you and God are one," the voice challenged, "you could jump off of this temple and not be harmed. After all, doesn't the Bible say that angels are always around to protect you?"

Jesus' divine spirit responded, "There would be only one reason to challenge my Heavenly Father in this way, and that would be to prove that I am uniquely loved and protected. But that is not my mission. My purpose here on Earth is not to prove that I am more holy than anyone, but that God loves everyone the same way He loves me."

For the third test the voice of personal pride guided Jesus to a high mountaintop. "Look at what stands below you. Glorious cities that could be yours if you simply renounced your spirituality and focused all your attention on earthly desires instead."

Jesus' reply was swift and commanding. "Silence! I now realize that the lure of earthly temptation has only as much power as I choose to give it, so I will give it none! I will not serve two masters, and from this moment on my heart and mind will forever be focused on God, the infinite source of love and abundance."

With that, the test was over and the tempting voices fell silent.

It had come to pass that John the Baptist had been arrested, so picking up where John left off, Jesus began his own ministry in Galilee. In essence, his message was the same: "*Make the decision to restructure your life from the inside-out right now, because the Kingdom of Heaven is here for you to experience in this very moment!*"

One day, as Jesus walked along the beach of Lake Galilee, he happened upon two brothers, Simon (who would later be called Peter) and Andrew, who were fishing along the shore. Jesus stopped and said to them, "Why don't you come with me and I will show you how to become a new type of fisherman—a fisherman who catches souls instead of fish!" There must have been something intriguing about Jesus, for they both dropped their nets and followed him.

A little farther down the beach, the three of them came upon another pair of brothers, James and John, who were fishing on the lake. They were sitting in a boat mending their nets with their father Zebedee when Jesus approached and made them the same offer. Compelled by the invitation, the two men quickly left the boat and headed out to follow him.

From there Jesus went out actively preaching all over the area of Galilee. His message was always simple and direct; the Kingdom of Heaven is a state of being available to every person in every moment, not a place in the sky that can only be entered after death. Also, he healed people of disease and the negative effects of denying God's grace and love for everyone. Word spread quickly through all of Syria, and he was presented with every kind of ailment imaginable. Soon, people from all over Jerusalem, Judea and Jordan came to witness the miraculous deeds of Jesus.

Reflections

This chapter represents one of the most significant moments in Jesus' life and ministry, yet I believe it is also one of the most misunderstood. In the classic telling, Jesus wanders the desert meditating and fasting for 40 days before being greeted by Satan, who has come to test Jesus' spiritual resolve. During three different trials, Satan makes offers of comfort, safety, fame and fortune; all for the price of denouncing God.

While the story plays out like a classic morality tale of good versus evil, we have actually been invited by John the Baptist (and later Jesus himself) to view this encounter in a completely different way. If you remember, when John baptized people in the Jordan River, he made it very clear that what we call Heaven is not some place outside of us, but rather an internal state of being accessible to each and every person.

In this chapter, we are being invited to consider that, if Heaven is residing within us, doesn't it stand to reason that Hell may be as well? If so, this story presents us with a defining event in Jesus' life, because it is the moment when he realizes that the voices of temptation, separation, doubt and pride are not coming from somewhere outside of himself, but from within. He comes to understand that he is not subject to the prodding of external demons, but is personally responsible for his own thoughts, perceptions, words and deeds. I find it significant that the story of this internal spiritual battle comes before any of Jesus' teachings or prophecies, implying that we all must come to a similar declaration of sovereignty before our spiritual journey can truly begin.

There is another significant detail regarding this tale of temptation—it happens only once in any account of Jesus' life and ministry. In some spiritual communities today, there is a weighty notion of "shadow work," which is based on the presumption that if we do not routinely clear the darkness of our past or the evils surrounding our present, we cannot attain a higher state of spiritual awareness. I have met many people who seem proud of how much shadow work they have not only done, but continue to do on a regular basis.

Yet, if we take note of Jesus' example, we see that once we address, acknowledge and neutralize the darker aspects of ourselves, we do not need to keep repeating the process. It is a pivotal juncture in Jesus' life when he proclaims that, from this moment on, he will no longer empower any feelings of separation, temptation, fear or pride.

There is a well-known Native American story where a young warrior is mentally tormented and seeks the council of the tribe's medicine man. After listening to the brave's description of symptoms, the healer tells him that there are two powerful wolves residing within him: one which is noble and gentle, the other evil and violent. He goes on to say that, eventually, only one of them will survive.

When the brave nervously asks which wolf will live, the medicine man responds, "The one you nurture and feed."

There are many similar tales of this internal struggle found in spiritual teachings from cultures all over the world, but the story of Jesus encountering and forever laying his personal demons to rest gives us a unique glimpse of what life looks like after evil has been forever banished.

CHAPTER FIVE

Cause and Effect

With his reputation as a gifted prophet and healer growing rapidly, Jesus, along with his new disciples, walked towards a low hill in the countryside of northern Israel. Before long, a crowd began to gather around them, so they climbed the hillside for some peace and quiet. Soon after, Jesus spoke words that affected his apprentices deeply:

"I want you to reconsider the role of suffering in your life, because the fact is, you are closest to God when you're at the end of your own rope. Loss and crisis force you to release your attachments to the material world, and when there is less of your earthly self to worry about, there is more room for your spiritual self to grow and flourish.

"People who seem meek are actually the ambassadors and guides to the coming new era of peace and unity on Earth.

"If you yearn for deeper spiritual awareness, it will come to you to the degree you are willing to surrender and receive it. There is no effort.

"Celebrate if you are a person who is merciful, for to the extent you show compassion, compassion is shown back to you. Hear me clearly on this, because this is a key universal law. Whichever way you choose to treat others, you attract the same type of treatment for yourself. Is it logical to expect anything else?

"You are blessed when your heart is open and your authentic soul is pure, for it is then that you stop chasing the need to be admired and accepted by anyone else.

"Live your life in peace, for it is the peacemakers who know God more intimately.

"Your commitment to living a spiritual life will not always be a perfect fit with your earthly life, for in many ways they are two completely different things. Understand this, but don't let it get you down. At some point on your journey, negative reactions to your beliefs will be the catalyst that makes them stronger.

"Now is the time to decide who you're trying to serve with your life; a superficial and fickle society, or your loving Creator. To be sure, the more right your action is with God, the less commonplace it will be to those around you. Let this be the gauge of your conduct here on Earth."

The tone of his sermon became more intimate and tender. "Let me tell you why you're here. You are here on Earth to serve as God's seasoning salt. Do you understand the analogy? Salt brings out the true flavor of any food, just as your lives may serve to bring out the true nature of God to others. But if you lose your saltiness, what good are you?

"Or look at it this way: You are like lamps unto the world, and what is the very purpose of a lamp? To shine! Light brings colors to life and chases darkness away. You wouldn't light a candle and then cover it with a bucket, would you? Once you have decided that you are the embodiment of God's light and love, you should be the brightest light you can possibly be!

"Now, maybe you are wondering if my words contradict scriptures that have been written before, but I'm telling you as plainly as possible that they do not. If anything, my words *complete* what has been recounted through the ages. The story that has been playing out here on Earth needs to be concluded, and I know the ending the author has in mind. For the moment, rest easy knowing that there is a force at work supporting everything and every person that has ever existed, and that force is love.

"You can take this message lightly or seriously, but beware the consequences of your thoughts and actions. Be stingy with the law of love and you will find yourself pleading and clawing for it from others. But if you are generous and compassionate, you are inviting the same type of treatment to come to you. Hear me clearly; the high priests who don't practice what they preach are doomed to a life of misery! How could it be otherwise?

"You probably know and heed the ancient command to never murder anyone, but don't take this statement too casually. In the simplest of terms, understand that every single one of your thoughts, words and deeds is either supporting someone or tearing them down. Can't you see how being angry at someone or belittling a friend actually sucks the life out of them? The truth is, your words alone can injure and kill.

"Here's an example of how you should conduct yourself. Before you go to temple or make an offering, first go and make things right with anyone whom you might have wronged or who might have wronged you. Once this is done, then you are in the space to make things right with God.

"Or say you see an old enemy out on the street one day. Take it upon yourself to reconcile—don't wait for them to make the first move. Take charge and work things out or risk being the victim of the other person's wrath.

"I am sure you're aware of another commandment: '*Don't commit acts of infidelity*,' but it goes deeper than that. If you outwardly brag about your virtue but commit adultery in your mind, you are still guilty of adultery. It is the heart that gets corrupted when you break the bonds of a relationship, and your heart is just as easily polluted by your thoughts as it is your deeds. I know this isn't easy, but if you truly want to live a moral life, you have to consider yourself blind to immoral acts. Trust me, it would be better to live out your days with this type of limited vision than with perfect vision that is corrupt. The same goes for your actions. You'd be better off without the use of your hands than to have hands capable of any atrocity.

"And don't take divorce too lightly. The written laws might say you have done your legal duty if you get the proper paperwork, but a divorce does not clear you of your obligations to the person who was once your wife or husband, the person who is the mother or father of your children, the person you vowed before God to love forever.

"Be careful with your words, and don't ever say anything you don't really mean. This way, you won't have to worry about creating diversions and cover-ups later on. And don't bring spiritual jargon into a conversation if your heart's not in it. Don't say, 'I'll pray for you,' or 'God is with you,' if you're not being sincere. Empty words of piety just cheapen what you're really trying to say.

"Here's another old saying that really needs some clarification: '*An eye for an eye and tooth for a tooth.*' This may sound fair and rational, but where does it end? Though you may not want to hear it, here's how you should conduct yourselves; If someone hits you, stand there and take it, and then forgive them. If you've been sued in court and lost, part with the judgment gracefully—even thankfully—and get on with your life. If you have been taken advantage of, use that experience to stretch your patience and tolerance. Forget about justice and revenge and go about living your life guided by generosity and compassion.

"You've heard the expression *'Love your friends,'* but I challenge that notion. Instead, you should love not only your friends, but your enemies as well! Let the challenges they bring forth reveal the best in you, not the worst. If someone is giving you trouble, respond with compassion and prayer for them, for this is the most God-like response there is. When the sun shines or the rain falls, it does so for the good of everyone, not just those deserving such favor. If all you do is love those who are easy to love, what does that say about you? Anybody can do that! And if you show affection by doing nothing more than giving someone a smile, does that make you something special? The most despicable humans on Earth can do this much!

"To put it as simply as possible, I'm telling every one of you that you are all ambassadors of God and should boldly live your lives as such. Be loving and generous and gracious to others, the way God is with you."

REFLECTIONS

Although the "Sermon on the Mount" is Jesus' first documented oration to a crowd, it quickly becomes apparent that he is speaking from a place of deep wisdom and authority. His words convey an awareness of how the universe works, which in turn reveals a fundamental understanding of certain principles of physics and nature.

For example, when Jesus says that thinking adulterous thoughts is the same as committing adultery, he is revealing an important aspect of the quantum realm. As we now know, our bodies—especially our brains—run on and emit electrical energy, and of course it was Einstein who realized that energy and mass are interchangeable in his famous equation, *E=MC2*. With this being true, we must acknowledge that the thoughts that light up our brains are indeed real things that have a tangible effect on our lives. As such, when Jesus said that thinking something is as real as doing something, he was tapping into one of the more mysterious aspects of our existence.

In another quote, Jesus says that how you perceive and choose to conduct your life actually shapes the physical world around you. If you are cruel to people, you are likely to encounter similarly cruel people. When you are loving and kind, you attract love and kindness from others.

This is not chance. In the realm of physics, this phenomenon is known as *sympathetic resonance*, and is easily proven by conducting a simple experiment using multiple tuning forks. In the experiment, a fork of a specific frequency is placed in the middle of all the others, of which only one is tuned to match the exact frequency of the one in the middle. What we discover is that, when the central fork is struck, its vibration activates only the one tuned to the same frequency, while every other fork remains motionless and silent. This intriguing result provides an example of the way our energy activates the same potential vibration in others. Whether you radiate anger or love, joy or sorrow, you should not be surprised to find yourself surrounded by people who mirror the same frequency as you. This is a fundamental aspect of Jesus' teachings, and it is astonishing that its principle is validated by discoveries made in modern science.

Later in the sermon, Jesus addresses the concepts of justice, fairness and punishment. In his time, the most fair and just laws regarding personal conduct were based on the Code of Hammurabi, an ancient Babylonian text which judiciously doled out either equal reward for a kind act or punishment matching the severity of a crime. One would not reciprocate a precious gift with one of scant value, just as a person who stole a loaf of bread would not suffer the same sentence as someone who had committed murder. What we learn in this passage is that Jesus' teachings transcend Hammurabi's "*eye for an eye*" legal system and are instead grounded in the unwavering principle of love above all else.

In many ways, the concept of justice has evolved greatly over the past two millennia, yet the laws of radical kindness, forgiveness and compassion spoken by Jesus are as challenging to live by today as they were when he spoke them. We still believe in punishment equal to a crime, and we judge harshly someone who does not reciprocate gratitude in equal measure of a gift. We do this because we are compelled to try to control our environment, as well as the people around us, based on the assumption that our world would slip into chaos if there were no rules governing human behavior. This may be true, but Jesus was not talking about the rules of Earth. He was talking about aligning with and preparing ourselves for the Kingdom of Heaven, a state of being where infinite compassion and unconditional love reign supreme. In this realm, which he described as being available to every person in every now moment, all sins are forgiven and no one is ever unloved.

CHAPTER SIX

The Trappings of Spirituality

"Be careful as you go out with your good intentions, for it is easy to lose your focus and start worrying about the impression you are making rather than living a moral life for its own sake. Don't make a performance out of your righteous behavior because God, the only audience to your actions who really matters, won't be applauding. When you do something kind for someone, don't make a spectacle out of it. We've all seen the show-offs who do things for admiration, but that's a fleeting thing. When you commit and act of kindness, do it as a true expression of who you really are and don't worry about who sees it. This is exactly how God works in your life.

"And when you pray, don't get theatrical. God is not critiquing your acting, He is listening to the genuine voice of your heart. Here are some suggestions for you when you pray: Find a quiet place, take a few deep breaths, and let yourself be as still as possible as you invite holiness into the moment. The world is full of charlatans who make a big production out of prayer, full of advice on how to manipulate God into giving you everything you want. Don't fall for that nonsense! This is God we are talking about here! Do you think He doesn't already know exactly what you need? Instead, make your prayer simple and heart-felt, something like this:

Dear Heavenly Father,

I love and honor You to the depth of my being!

Every aspect of creation reveals Your design and will,

As above, so below. As within, so without.

Thank You for providing me with everything I need to thrive.

Assist me in forgiving others the same way You always forgive me.

Hold me in the service of love and help me find my way out of error.

I see how Your power and glory keep all things in motion and balance.

I am eternally grateful for this life You have given me!

"In prayer, there is an intimate spiritual bond between you and your Creator, and the strength of this bond has much more to do with how you live your life than the words you say. Don't even bother asking for forgiveness if you can't find it in your heart to forgive others. Your relationship with Spirit is a two-way street.

"If you decide to fast to help you focus your attention on spiritual development, do so privately and with humility. If you are far along on your spiritual journey, make sure people still recognize you as their path crosses yours. God sees you always and is not impressed by grandiose displays of self-righteousness.

"Don't spend all your energy acquiring and hoarding material possessions here on Earth, where they rust and rot or can be stolen. Start building your spiritual nest egg for your life in Eternity, where nothing can happen to your treasure. Do you see how it works? Where you place your attention and care, there you will be drawn.

"Your external reality mirrors your perspective. If you open your mind's eye in grateful wonder to beauty and kindness, more will fill your vision. But if you believe that the world is a dangerous place, life will prove to be as threatening as you fear it to be. If you choose to pull the blinds down and hide in fear, you may do so... but what a dark and small existence you will live. You may not fully understand or appreciate the significance of this, but know that God not only gives you the free will to choose how you perceive the world, the entire universe conspires to support your perceptions! Are you beginning to understand what a powerful creator you are of your life both here on Earth and in the eternal realm of Heaven?

"You cannot worship two gods at once, for if you fully love one, you will fully ignore the other. You can't worship God and material wealth at the same time. If you choose to live a life pursuing God, it follows that you will not also be absorbed with eating gourmet food or wearing the most fashionable clothes. There is so much more to you than the type of food you eat or the clothes you wear. Consider the birds—care-free and yet completely cared-for by God, and you are so much more valuable to God than a bird.

"Will obsessing in front of a mirror do anything to change the real you? Don't concern yourself with fashion trends that are here today and gone tomorrow. Why get caught up in that nonsense? Instead, try walking out into a field of wildflowers.

They never shop or fuss, but have you ever seen such beauty and color? The best-dressed people in the world have nothing on these natural wonders!

"And if God pays so much attention to the beauty of these flowers, don't you think He would do that much more for someone as wonderful as you? What I'm saying is that you can relax and not strive so hard to receive what God is happy to freely give! Focus your attention on living an awakened life, don't worry about missing out on superficial validation, and you'll find yourself abundantly provided for in ways you may never have even considered.

"Live in the now, feel Spirit's presence in every moment, and don't worry about what may or may not happen tomorrow. If you do this much, God will always be with you to get you through whatever challenges life may bring."

Reflections

This portion of the Sermon on the Mount poignantly addresses society's often frantic quest for external gratification over the grounded, inward journey of divine awakening.

As Jesus shares this particular lesson with the people gathered at the bottom of the hill, he describes the connection between inner knowingness and spirituality. Modern Christianity often portrays self-awareness as a selfish, "new age" pursuit, yet Jesus' words remind us that, to truly awaken, we must first be genuine and authentic unto ourselves. It is interesting to note that both Buddha and Socrates, spiritual philosophers who lived centuries before Jesus, were firmly committed to the idea that "knowing thyself" was a fundamental aspect of living a spiritual life.

Continuing, Jesus provides the crowd with an example of how to pray. The words he speaks are now known all over the world as "the Lord's Prayer," a short but powerful invocation that is first and foremost a statement of gratitude to God for this incredible experience we call life. To me, this prayer also reveals Jesus' expanded sense of perception and awareness, where words like, "On Earth as it is in Heaven," (or, per my translation, "As above, so below") reflect a fundamental understanding of the quantum realm, where the same patterning can be observed in both the smallest and the largest organized structures in the universe. Whether it be the spiral of the tiniest snail or the spiral of an entire galaxy, there is an obvious similarity mirroring the micro and the macro in every aspect of creation. One could call this relationship "the thumbprint of God," and it can be found in everything and in every life.

Later, Jesus reiterates the importance of self-love and acceptance, making it clear that, only to the level that you are able to cherish and honor yourself are you able to do the same for others. Some people compare this philosophy to the oxygen-mask rule while flying, where, in an emergency, you are to first make sure you can breathe before trying to help anyone else around you. This is an oversimplified analogy, but it does get the idea across that, if you are not able to take care of yourself—which includes loving and forgiving—you won't be of much use to anyone else in need of love and forgiveness.

Following this, Jesus provides another pearl of wisdom that, if taken out of context, could be considered by many as blasphemous. When he says that the world mirrors every person's perception, he is implying that each one of us is actually the creator of our reality. We are beings who, through God's gift of free will, have the incredible ability to manifest our experience by choosing the way we view the world around us.

Lastly, Jesus addresses materialism, wealth and fame and how the pursuit of these things can serve as major roadblocks on our journey of spiritual awakening. In what could only be described as a paradox, we often idealistically align with spiritual teachings of humility, peace, service and compassion, yet our culture is more consumed by wealth, materialism, competition and fame than ever before.

Novelist John Steinbeck observed and wrote about this dichotomy. During a scientific and often philosophical ocean voyage he took with marine biologist Ed Ricketts in 1940, he came to realize that while the idealistic qualities of generosity and kindliness are what most humans would call "good," and traits such as greed and self-interest are often considered "bad," we never-the-less admire individuals who claw and fight their way to fortune and fame more than honest, humble and helpful people who possess little material wealth. In essence, what Steinbeck concluded is that most humans would rather be successful than good, a trait that his marine biologist friend would probably have said was similar to Darwin's notion of *"survival of the fittest."*

Jesus addresses this issue by stating that the frantic pursuit of wealth and fame is not only exhausting, it is the primary distraction standing in the way of our awakening. He does not go so far as to say that a person who strives for money is evil, but he certainly makes the point that the chase for riches and adulation is counter-productive to one's process of spiritual growth.

But what about those who are not obsessed with materialism, the people who just want enough food to sustain them and a roof over their head? Jesus has plenty to say about this as well, noting that worrying about anything—even the basic necessities such as food, clothing and shelter—can be just as detrimental to our connection with Spirit as being fixated on buying an expensive car or home. In poetic fashion, he assures us that, just as the birds and flowers are cared for by God, so too are we provided with everything we need to thrive.

CHAPTER SEVEN

The Law of Attraction

"Don't criticize other people, unless of course you would like to receive the same type of criticism. Can't you see that, by drawing attention to a person's minor flaw, you are revealing an even greater flaw in yourself? It's a superficial role you're playing and you're not fooling anyone. Work on your own issues first, and then, maybe, you'll be able to offer someone else a piece of constructive advice.

"Don't be flippant with your spirituality. Trends and slogans have their place, but that place is not with God. Don't reduce the mysteries of the universe into superficial jargon and catchphrases. By trying to be cutting-edge and relevant, you may actually be deflecting attention away from Spirit.

"Avoid trying to make deals with your Heavenly Father. When you need something, be direct and pray for it in the purest terms possible. Does anything else even make sense? If your child asked you for a slice of bread, would you give him a block of wood instead? If he asked for fish for dinner, would you offer him a live snake? As a parent looking out in the best interest of your child, of course you would do neither of these things. Doesn't it stand to reason that your Father in Heaven would provide you with everything you need?

"Here's a simple guideline for you: Treat everyone the way you would want to be treated. If you summarize all the prophesies and ancient teachings of God's Law, this is the point they make.

"There is no way to beat the system in regards to leading a spiritual life. The world is full of enticing and easy paths to spirituality, but don't fall for them. Listen to your heart and follow its call to always do the right thing, which is rarely the easiest thing.

"Be aware that there are many false prophets and spiritual predators. You'll know them by their thin veneer of holiness, which just barely covers their true desire for fame, money, and power. Get past their words and validate them instead by their actions. Real teachers won't take advantage of you or pressure you into giving them money. False teachers have chosen the temporary trappings of celebrity status and wealth over an everlasting relationship to God, which is a very foolish choice indeed.

"Reciting lofty words will not get you closer to God if those words are not backed up by action. I can just see it now, when the end of this order comes, all those who will come to me and claim how holy they were. 'Weren't we impressive in our godliness?' they'll ask. Which I will have to reply, 'No. All you were really doing was puffing yourselves up with personal pride, and that way of thinking has no place in God's realm, whether it be in Heaven or here on Earth.'

"What I'm telling you here is not trivial information or some kind of last-minute addition to the way you should live your life. These words are the very foundation to build your life upon, and you would be wise to do so, just as a wise carpenter builds his house on a solid foundation of rock so it won't be washed away by the first rainstorm.

"But if you just listen to my words and choose not to act on them, you will be like a foolish carpenter who decides to build his house on sand. It doesn't take a genius to figure out that his house will crumble and be swept away when the rains come."

When Jesus finished his sermon, people applauded, for they had never heard a message like this. It was apparent to them that he was indeed living the words he was speaking, which was very different than the way their esteemed religious teachers conducted themselves. No one could deny that this was the most inspiring and instructive message about God they had ever heard.

Reflections

As he concludes his sermon, Jesus boldly reveals a different kind of Heavenly Father to the people of Israel. Up to this point, Jews have been the subjects of a wrathful and jealous God. But standing before them is a humble prophet describing a loving Father who bestows upon His children the freedom and tools needed to create their own life experience.

The awareness that I am the person most responsible for my reality came to me in my early 20s, when I first read Dr. Wayne Dyer's, *Your Erroneous Zones*. I had not previously read such a personally empowering book, and I will never forget my favorite quote from it: "Be miserable. Or motivate yourself. Whatever has to be done. It is always your choice." I took this to mean, "While you are always free to wallow in misery and self-pity, never forget that you also have the option of being happy." Reading this reminded me that I deserved and was already equipped with everything I needed to live a meaningful, fulfilling and joyful life. Now, over forty years later, I can say that while I am neither monetarily rich or famous, my days are filled primarily with happiness, purpose, and gratitude.

Dyer's quote regarding the power of choice also brings into focus what many people have come to know as "The Law of Attraction." While some people familiar with this term think it means that we can just mentally focus on something we desire and it will magically come into being, Jesus finds many ways to say that the true Law of Attraction is not some cosmic parlor trick. Rather, it is a force of nature conspiring to support the choices we make. And this is where we begin to realize that the universe must always abide by its own laws, which means it will support our perceptions, regardless of what those perceptions happen to be.

There is a saying, "Be careful what you wish for," but the universe is already aware of what you are expecting from it by the way you have chosen to live your life. For instance, if you are in the habit of criticizing others, you are most likely not consciously hoping to be criticized the same way, but what other outcome could there be? If you are willing to step on people to acquire something, how could you not be living in a world where others would do the same to you? This is the real law of attraction, where what you habitually think, say and do are the primary forces shaping your reality.

One of the most important and recurring lessons in Jesus' ministry is that we should treat people the way we want to be treated. This simple teaching affirms that you and I are the creators, not the victims, of our life experience. Be the type of person you wish to encounter, and you will encounter more of those types of people. Live in gratitude and more will come for which you can be grateful. Be of service and you will find yourself being served in your moments of need. The Law of Attraction is not complicated, but it is consequential, so be very aware of what it is you are both consciously and subconsciously allowing into your field of awareness.

CHAPTER EIGHT

As You Believe

As Jesus left the crowd, a leper approached him and threw himself down on the ground saying, "Master, if you wanted to, I know you could heal my body."

Tenderly, Jesus touched the man and said, "I want to, you are healed." At that moment, all signs of leprosy were gone. Then Jesus added, "Don't share with others what just happened here. Instead, I want you to go to a priest and express to him your thankfulness for God's gift of healing. Your gratitude will best represent what I have done for you today."

Later, when Jesus entered the town of Capernaum, a Roman captain rushed up to him in a panic and said, "Master, my servant is sick. He can't walk and he is in terrible pain."

"Then I will come and heal him," Jesus replied.

"Please, no," said the captain. "I don't want to put you out like that. I know that if you just give the order, my servant will be fine.

It's just like being in the army: If I give the order to a soldier to go, he goes, and if I tell another to come, he comes. The same holds true with my slaves."

Jesus was amazed by the Roman's response. "I don't receive this kind of trust even from the people of Israel, the very ones who supposedly know all there is to know about God! This man is among the first of many gentiles who will come and bear witness to God's word in action. And those who grew up in the faith but in fact have no real faith will find themselves wandering in darkness, disillusioned that their strict religion was not aligned with Spirit after all."

Then Jesus said to the captain, "You can go now. What you have believed to be true has already happened; your servant is well."

Not long after this, Jesus arrived with a few others to Peter's house. Upon entering, they found Peter's mother to be bedridden with a dangerously high fever. With just a touch from Jesus' hand, the fever broke and soon she was up on her feet preparing dinner for them!

Later that evening, people with afflictions of every kind were brought to Jesus and he healed them all, which brought to life the well-known sermon of Isaiah, which stated, *"He took our illness. He carried our diseases."*

When Jesus noticed how large the crowd was becoming, he told his disciples to figure out a way to get him to the other side of the lake. As they were leaving, a religious scholar asked if he could go with them. "I'll follow wherever you lead," said the man.

Jesus was straightforward with him. "Are you sure you could live the way we do? After all, we don't stay at nice hotels on our travels."

Another follower spoke up. "Master, my father just died and I need to attend to his funeral plans. If you could just give me a couple of days, I will then follow you."

But Jesus declined the offer. "Get your priorities straight, my friend. Your new pursuit is life, not death. Follow my teachings and live life to the fullest."

Soon after boarding the boat that would take them across the lake, a raging storm began to blow and churned the waters violently. Waves were crashing all around them, yet Jesus was fast asleep. Fearing for their lives, the disciples roused him shouting, "Save us! We're sinking!"

Jesus opened his eyes and spoke sternly to them. "What are you afraid of? Are you that faint-hearted?" He then calmly arose and walked to the edge of the boat, meditating on his connectedness to everything in nature, even the windswept waters of Galilee. As he stood there, he breathed quietly and allowed his spirit to become one with the sea. "Be still," he called out, and to the astonishment of those around him, the waters did in fact become still.

The men in the boat could hardly believe what they had seen. "How could this be? Even the wind and sea respond to his command!"

Without further incident they landed in the country of the Gadarenes, where they were met by two wild swineherds who had taken up residence in a nearby cemetery. The men had haunted the place for so long that no one traveled near there for fear of being attacked. But upon seeing Jesus and feeling his divine spirit, they called out, "What are you doing here? Our wickedness cannot exist amidst your purity!"

Off in the distance their herd of pigs was rooting around for food. The men, convinced that they were under the influence of demons, pleaded, "Release these evil spirits and let them reside in those pigs over there."

"As you wish," Jesus replied. With that, the herd became crazed and stampeded over a cliff into the sea and drowned. Astonished and frightened, the men ran back to the village and told everyone what had happened. But rather than being impressed, the crowd was angry at the loss of the pigs and demanded that Jesus leave at once.

REFLECTIONS

In the Star Wars movie, *The Empire Strikes Back*, a young Luke Skywalker is guided to the planet Dagobah, where he is to begin his training as a Jedi. When he crash-lands into a swamp, he is amazed that Master Yoda is able to levitate his X-wing fighter out of the murky water and maneuver it safely onto dry land.

"I don't believe it!" Skywalker gasps as he watches his craft float through the air.

"That is why you fail," Yoda responds with a deep sigh.

I find it interesting that, depending on the circumstance, the word "belief" can be used as an example of either weakness or empowerment. To some, believing something may or may not happen is akin to wishing or hoping, a passive stance negating the power of determination and action.

Yet to those in the field of quantum science, research suggests that a person's belief is often the very thing which sets the stage for a particular result. There is a classic experiment called "the double-slit phenomenon" which, when it was first conducted by British polymath Thomas Young in the early 1800s, revealed that light—much like sound—is wave-like in nature.

Today, this experiment is conducted by projecting high-intensity light through two parallel slits in a flat surface and taking note of the pattern it reveals. As Thomas' first discovered, after the light passes through the slits, it will curiously project many wavelike lines fading laterally away from each other.

However, when the test is conducted under the watchful eye of an observer, the light is found to be made of particles that arrange themselves in accordance to what most people would expect to see—only the two slits. This incredible phenomenon not only proves that light can be both a wave and a particle, but that these tiny particles are somehow *aware* when they are being observed and *choose* to conform to the beliefs and expectations of the observer conducting the experiment!

Though Jesus lived in a time when mythology, magic and superstition stood for much of the science of the day, he seemed to grasp certain scientific principles that would not be proven for nearly 2,000 years. In this chapter, we begin to sense his ability to not only comprehend what we now call quantum mechanics, but also how it affects the human experience. Specifically, he realized that belief is a crucial component regarding a person's receptivity to healing. Otherwise, there would have been no reason for him to ask people if they believed they could be healed.

Today, this connection between belief and physical healing is often referred to as the "placebo effect," a rather dismissive term used to explain how someone who believes they have taken an effective medication—even if that medication is later revealed to be nothing more than a sugar pill—is often cured of their ailment. This profound and mysterious phenomenon linking belief to physical manifestation suggests the way the quantum universe works.

Later, when Jesus departs on a boat with his disciples, we are introduced to the unified-field condition known as *entanglement*. As physicists are becoming more aware, all things are not only made up of subatomic particles of energy, they are intertwined with one another to form one giant organism we call the universe. To imagine this, try touching fingers with a friend and visualizing your connection through a microscope so powerful it can reveal subatomic particles. What you quickly realize is that the distinction between the two of you has become an overlapping lattice of protons and electrons, making it impossible to see where your finger ends and your friend's finger begins. It is in this field that everything is not only connected to, but also has an effect upon, everything else.

For all his brilliance, Albert Einstein was still mystified by the behavior of the tiniest particles of what we call matter. For instance, when he was presented the idea that two once-conjoined photons could *instantaneously* behave identically to one another regardless of how far apart they are, the only term he could come up with to describe this phenomenon was "spooky action at a distance."

Any ideas we have of separation come from the limited way we perceive our reality—I am different and separate from you, a tree is separate from the ground, a bee is separate from a flower. Yet to the mind of philosopher Alan Watts, the idea of separation was a hazy one, whereas a bee could not exist without flowers for nectar, and flowers could not exist without bees for pollinating. From this conclusion, Watts understood that what was really being presented to him was the organism "bee-flower," and yet even this binary life form was found to be connected with everything else into infinity: bee-flower to water, water to animal life, animal life to intelligence, intelligence to all creation.

There are stories of indigenous people feeling so connected to their environment that they actually have a sense of *being* the environment itself. When asked if it is going to rain, they drop deeply into this connection and reply with an unexpected answer: "Let me check, do I feel like I am going to rain?" From here, we can see that rituals like Native American rain dances are not pleas for precipitation, rather they are celebrations acknowledging that everything has an influence on everything else.

In a similar way, we can almost feel Jesus dropping into this same deep state of awareness as the storm-swept seas toss the boat he and his disciples are in. If we imagine this moment taking place in a cosmically entangled universe, we can begin to see that not only does a storm affect human life, but human life can affect—and even calm—a storm.

Chapter Nine

The Nature of Miracles

Back in the boat, Jesus and his disciples returned to Galilee. They had barely disembarked when a paraplegic, brought down to them in a stretcher carried by other men, was placed at Jesus' feet. Taken aback by this bold statement of belief, Jesus said, "Don't worry, my friend. Sin has no power to do this to you, for your sins are always forgiven."

Some nearby religious scholars interpreted this to mean that Jesus' personal forgiveness was what would make the man well. "Blasphemy!" they challenged.

Jesus wanted to make clear that he wasn't proclaiming to be anything other than an earthly ambassador of God's love and forgiveness. He said, "Why are you projecting into my words? After all, which do you think is simpler to say, 'Your sins are forgiven' or, 'Take up your mat and walk out of here?' Well, to demonstrate to you that I am as close to God as a son is to his father, I will say it both ways: My friend, know that your sins are indeed always forgiven and you may now take up your mat and walk." Immediately the man rose to his feet and did as he was told. The crowd that had gathered around them was amazed and delighted to see God work through Jesus in this way.

As they continued ahead, Jesus noticed a man named Matthew collecting taxes. "Let's walk together," Jesus said, and Matthew got up and followed him.

Later, Jesus and his disciples were dining at Matthew's house when a rough and boisterous bunch of people decided to join them. When the religious leaders saw Jesus dining comfortably with this group, they could hardly stand it. "What kind of example is your master setting by hanging out with these low-lifes?" they asked his disciples.

Jesus overheard them and fired back, "Who would you say needs a doctor most; one who is healthy, or one who is sick? Go back and study the meaning of this scripture: *'I am here to share God's love with those who are in need of it, not pander to religious elitists.'*

A while later some holy men stepped up and asked, "Why do we and the Pharisees discipline ourselves by fasting, while you and your followers do not?"

Jesus answered them directly. "When you celebrate a wedding, you don't withhold the wine and cake, do you? And no one would throw water on a celebratory bonfire, would they? Well, if you were waiting for The Kingdom of Heaven to arrive before celebrating, I'm telling you to wait no longer. The Kingdom of Heaven is here for you to experience in this very moment."

He continued, "Nobody would rip up a fine silk scarf to use as patches for tattered old clothes, and you wouldn't store good wine in cracked bottles, right?"

Just as he finished speaking, a local official came into the room and said, "My daughter has just died. But I know that if you come and touch her, she will live." At hearing this, Jesus got up and with his disciples followed the man.

As they walked along, a woman afflicted with chronic internal bleeding slipped in amongst them and lightly touched Jesus' robe. Her thought was that if she just touched his cloak, she would be healed. Jesus felt the intent of the suffering woman and said, "Have courage, dear sister. Led by your faith you took a risk, and now you are well." Indeed, the woman was immediately made well and her bleeding stopped.

By now they had made their way to the official's house, and they had to push their way past the well-wishers and gossips. "Get out of here," Jesus commanded them. "This girl is not dead, she is just sleeping." Everyone there mocked him, as it was obvious that the girl was indeed deceased. But after the crowd left, Jesus went to the girl and, taking her hands in his, gently pulled her up and steadied her on her feet! Of course, the news of this miracle spread like wildfire throughout the region.

Just as Jesus was leaving the house, two blind men approached him pleading, "Please have mercy on us!" Jesus led them back to the home where he was staying and asked them, "Do you really believe this miracle can happen; that your sight can be restored?"

They answered enthusiastically, "Yes, master, we do!"

At that, Jesus touched their eyes and said, "Then live your belief and be healed." With that, both men were able to see. Before they left, Jesus warned them not to share with anyone what had just happened, but it was not long before they were telling everyone about the miracle that had taken place.

Later, a mute was presented to Jesus and he, too, was instantly healed. All who witnessed the results of these healings exclaimed, "There has never been anyone in all of Israel who could do such things!"

Jewish leaders of the area took a different view. "This is nothing but quackery or, worse, dark magic of some kind. This man Jesus has probably made a pact with Satan to be able to do such things."

Jesus' ministry flourished throughout the area. Daily he taught and healed and spread the joyful news that The Kingdom of Heaven was upon them if they would just open their hearts and minds to the fact. But as he looked out over the crowds, he could see how spiritually aimless and lost they were. "There is such a need," he said to his disciples, "yet so few of us to help fulfill it! Pray that you could be a part of these people's spiritual awakening!"

Reflections

As Jesus moves more confidently into his abilities as a healer, he proves himself to be something more than the product of his Jewish upbringing. He defies many of Judaism's strict regulations and constantly reminds ordinary citizens that they are just as close to God as any high-ranking religious official.

Today, we can see how some religions function like corporate or militaristic organizations, where lowly recruits are expected to revere and obey the more accomplished above them. By contrast, Jesus reveals that the Heavenly Realm is a state of being where there is no vertical organization-chart—a place where one does not have to start at the bottom and work their way up.

It is a telling moment when Jesus addresses a leper who is no longer able to walk. As the sick man is obviously under the impression that his evil past is the cause of this pitiful state, Jesus reminds the man that, even if this were true, his sins are always forgiven and therefore he may take his mat and walk away.

Jewish scholars within earshot of this exchange are shocked by what they are hearing. How can some lowly drifter claim to do what only God—or at least a high priest of their religion—can do?

Once again, Jesus finds a powerful way to demonstrate that, as children of the same loving Creator, every person on Earth is always intimately connected to the very Source of love and forgiveness. Of course, this outrages the priests, for if everyone can have full and instant access to God, what need is there for the venerated leaders of a synagogue or church?

In another encounter, the priests ask why it's all right for Jesus to dine and celebrate with his friends and disciples, while they starve themselves for the glory of God?

In his allegorical way, Jesus reminds them that if they are waiting to celebrate the arrival of the Kingdom of Heaven, they need wait no longer. He makes it clear that Heaven is not a place in the sky being guarded over by an angry and vengeful God, but a glorious realm that every person can experience while still here on Earth. As such, there is no need to wait to celebrate the awareness that we are all children of the Father, that divinity resides in every one of us, and that we are all creators capable of manifesting miracles in our lives.

CHAPTER TEN

Leave Your Ego Behind

Before long, Jesus decided to disperse his disciples to share spiritual truths with all who were ready to receive them. The twelve he chose were: Simon (who would later be known as Peter) and his brother Andrew, bothers James and John, Phillip, Bartholomew, Thomas, Matthew the tax collector, another man called James, Thaddaeus, Simon, and Judas.

Jesus sent them out with instructions. "Don't start your ministries by traveling to distant lands to convert non-believers, and don't grandstand by challenging high-profile leaders. No, look for the lost in your own back yard and tell them that the eternal Kingdom of Heaven can be found in every moment of their lives. Heal them, share God's love with them, raise them from the dead, touch those whom no one else will touch, and ease their afflictions. You are all as capable as me to do these things, so do not be afraid to do them.

"And don't think this has to be a grandiose or complicated mission. This isn't some expensive political campaign you're on. Don't even bother taking a lot of equipment with you, for *you* are the equipment, and all you need to keep functioning is a little food and water.

"When you travel to other towns, don't worry about staying in the nicest inns. Find a simple place amongst modest people and be happy with that.

"As you're out spreading the good news to people, be courteous to them. If they welcome you, be gentle and gracious in return. If they do not welcome you, don't make a fuss, just move on. Those people have made an unwise choice and will pay for it accordingly, but that is no concern of yours.

"Stay on your toes, for this mission will be dangerous at times. You are going to be like sheep running through a pack of wolves, so don't draw too much attention to yourselves. Be as cunning as snakes and as delightful as doves.

"Be prepared. Some people will challenge your motives, others will try to ruin your reputation just because you believe in the teachings I have shared with you. Don't get mad when they drag you in front of their civic leaders, for without knowing it, they have actually helped your mission by providing you a larger audience. And don't be concerned about what you're going to say or how you're going to say it; God's Spirit will pass through you and deliver just what needs to be heard at the moment.

"Know that the people you will meet have been worshipping many gods and idols for a long time. The idea that there is a singular Source of Grace will not be eagerly embraced, and they will very likely turn on you. Ironic, isn't it? Here you are delivering a message of God's infinite love and all you get in return is hate. But don't get discouraged, for this is the most important thing you will ever do. It is not earthly success you are after; this quest is one of spiritual awakening. And just when you think you're out of options, know that God is always with you.

"A student doesn't get better supplies than the teacher, and a laborer doesn't make more money than his boss, right? In that regard, be happy when you get the same poor treatment I have received. If people call me foul names, would you expect less for yourselves?

"Don't get intimidated. Soon enough, all that I am telling you will be common knowledge to everyone, so don't be afraid to go public now.

"And don't let people bully you into silence. The worst they can do to you is take away your earthly life, but that has nothing to do with your eternal soul, so don't worry. Save your genuine concern for God, who will always provide for you.

"How much does a canary cost at the pet store? Hardly anything, right? Yet look at how well God cares for these little creatures, which is nothing in comparison to how much He cares for you. He knows everything about you, right down to the number of hairs on your head! So don't ever be afraid of bullies, for your eternal life is worth more than a million canaries to God.

"Stand up for me and the good news I'm sharing with the world, and I'll stand up for you before my Father in Heaven. If you deny the message I bring, what good would it do to defend you before the Father who knows everything about you?

"Don't assume that my message will bring about an earthly peace, because it won't—my mission is to disrupt stale dogma and tradition. Ancient notions about what it means to live a spiritual life will be pitted against my teachings, and blood relatives will find themselves in conflict over their beliefs. And if you should choose to cling to old ideas rather than God's truth, know that God will honor that choice and leave you alone to fend for yourselves.

"If you do not follow this message wholeheartedly, you don't deserve the gift that can only be earned through your willful compliance with the laws of Spirit. If your first concern is your earthly life, you can forget about your spiritual life. But if you can look past yourself and embody the message that I'm sharing, you will find both your earthly and spiritual lives fully realized.

"We are connected by the work that we're doing. Anyone who embraces what you tell them is accepting what I have told you. In the end, receiving God's message is as good as delivering it, and accepting someone's help is as good as giving it. This is a large undertaking, but don't be overwhelmed by it. Start small. Commit little acts of kindness along the way, which will validate to others your Heavenly Father's commission to you. Don't worry about changing the world overnight; this will happen in its course and you are all an integral participant in the process."

Reflections

This is the first chapter that mentions all 12 of Jesus' disciples by name, so it feels like the right moment to share the significance of the number 12 in geometry, physics, and ancient lore.

You may have heard of the Fibonacci Sequence, which produces an infinitely-expanding spiral based on a specific mathematical algorithm. As this elegantly simple pattern unfolds, the combined value of two previous numbers provides the sum and/ or volume of the next in the sequence (0, 1, 1, 2, 3, 5, 8 and so on). The geometric spiral this number sequence reveals is often referred to as "the fingerprint of God" because it can be found in the smallest of structures to the largest; from tiny seashells, to our physical bodies, to entire galaxies. Interestingly, the 12th position in the Fibonacci sequence happens to total 144, which is not only 12 squared, but is also a number sequence found in many religious texts, including the biblical Book of Revelation.

Did humanity's preoccupation with the number 12 come from recognizing it in nature, or is it significant to us now because it can be found in so many ancient texts and measuring systems all over the world? Consider the fact that, centuries before Jesus gathered 12 disciples to share his teachings, ancient Greeks and Romans both worshipped the same 12 gods, (even if the Romans did rename them). Additionally, our earliest ancestors decided to divide a year into 12 months, the zodiac into 12 constellations, a foot into 12 inches, and a day into 12 hours of light and 12 of darkness. Maybe Einstein was right when he said, "Coincidence is God's way of remaining anonymous."

In physics and advanced geometry, the concept of "12 around 1" takes the mystery one step further. It was back in the 1940s when Buckminster Fuller postulated that the entire universe may be a geometric matrix comprised of an energetic structure he called the "Vector Equilibrium," which consists of 12 perfectly balanced trajectories—all of equal length and angular offset—emanating from one "zero point" in the middle. It is fascinating to think that Jesus may have been innately aware of this structure and chose his "12 disciples gathered around 1" as a covert way to reveal his knowledge regarding the geometric model of the universe.

We don't know exactly how much time has passed from the moment Jesus recruited his disciples to when he sends them out on their own to minister, but we do know he is aware of the pitfalls and traps waiting for them when they embark on their mission.

Speaking to them as if they are a graduating class being sent out into the world, he cautions them to stay true to their mission and not be lured by material wealth and fame. Drawing from personal experience, he tells them not to worry about comfort or recognition, which can serve as distractions to living a spiritual life. He reminds them that they are not going out to impress others, but to model what it looks like to be of service to humanity. He also lets them know that they will be met with challenges, from people mocking them to living in physical discomfort, but that these trials should not discourage them.

And while the message they are to share is all about love and compassion, they should be ready to face an ironic backlash of hatred and scorn. Old ways and opinions die hard, so even though their mission is to deliver a message of God's grace, they should be prepared to be met with resistance and violence.

Before sending his disciples on their way, he reminds them not to expect any better treatment than he has so far received. However, he makes it clear that their efforts are not going to go unnoticed. God's universe is one that works on unwavering principles, and the journey they are about to embark upon is one that will provide them with many opportunities to recognize and release their earthly fears. He reminds them that the more they are ridiculed and physically threatened in the earthly realm, the more prepared they will be for the eternal Kingdom of Heaven.

CHAPTER ELEVEN

Earthly Frustration

After Jesus assigned the ministerial mission to his disciples, he ventured out himself and continued to preach the good news in local towns and villages.

During this time, John the Baptist had been arrested and sent to prison. While incarcerated, he got word about what Jesus was doing and sent out his own disciples to ask, "Are you the Messiah, the One who will deliver our people out of torment and persecution, or are we still waiting?"

Jesus replied, "Go and tell John what's been happening: The blind now see. The lame now walk. Lepers are cured. The deaf now hear. The dead have been raised. The lowliest people on earth have been made aware that God is always with them.

"Is this what you were expecting of a Messiah? If so, consider yourselves blessed to have seen me in action."

When John's followers left to report what they heard and saw, Jesus addressed the crowd gathered around him. "What were you expecting to find when you went down to the river to see John; a delusional madman? Of course not. A figure of royalty reclining in fancy robes? That hardly describes him, either. Then what was he, a prophet? That's exactly right, and probably the most insightful prophet any of you will ever know. He is the prophesier mentioned by Malachi who would be sent in advance of the one who will prepare the road ahead.

"Let me make myself as clear as possible; No human surpasses John the Baptist, but in Heaven, even the lowest are ahead of him. For those of you able to understand, John is the prophet Elijah, the one who would announce me to the world.

"How do I describe this generation of people? You are like scatterbrained children always twisting the truth. John came to you fasting and you called him crazy. I come to you feasting and you call me a glutton and a lush. In reality, your opinions don't count for anything, for you choose to ignore the obvious facts staring you in the face."

In a moment of agitation, Jesus let loose on some of the cities who had shunned his message and instead forged blindly ahead with their own beliefs. "You are doomed, Chorazin and Bethsaida. If more corrupt places had witnessed the miracles I performed in your towns, they would be praising God in earnest. Woe be to you when God bestows on you the very separation from Him you seem to desire! And Capernaum; with all your grandeur here on Earth, you have seen all the glory you'll ever know. If the people in the sleazy town of Sodom had had your chance, that city would still be around today. In God's judgment, those people were way better off than you are now, for they did not get the chance to hear the truth spoken so plainly."

Jesus stopped his tirade and began to focus his thoughts in prayer. "Thank you, Father, Creator of everything that ever was or will be. You have concealed the mysterious way You do things from the so-called experts, but have revealed Yourself to the innocent and the lowly. Yes, Father, I know this is how Your will is accomplished."

Now calm and filled with compassion, Jesus continued his sermon to the people. "My Heavenly Father has given me all these things to do and say, for God is the Father and I am the Son, and no one knows a Father like his Son, right? But hear me clearly: you are all children of the same Father, and many of you will share these teachings with the world.

"Are you tired and fed up with the pressures of life? Then listen to me and hear what God is offering you. Let your heart rest in the truth of what I'm saying and you will be refreshed in ways you never thought possible. Walk in my shoes, listen to my words, take heed of my actions and you will discover what it means to live a purposeful and peaceful life."

Reflections

I have a friend who hosts workshops for authors, and she has been instrumental in my various writing projects over the years. She grew up in a religious family, so I decided to get her feedback on this book while it was still a work in progress. When I reached out to her, I had not yet written any of these "reflections" following each chapter, which she and a few other friends suggested I add.

After she finished reading the draft, we met for lunch to talk about it. For the most part, she was enthusiastic about the project, but she wondered why I chose to make Jesus sound so angry and temperamental at times. This caught me off guard, because the references she mentioned were not inventions; they are all right there in the gospel. As you will read in the coming pages, there are many times when Jesus reveals his human frailties of frustration, anger, scorn and fear, but this is the first chapter which provides us a glimpse into how he manages them. The fact that Jesus has to deal with many of the same annoyances and trials as the rest of us makes him a more compelling spiritual teacher.

By comparison, it is said that after achieving total enlightenment, the Buddha never felt anger again in his life. He addressed and philosophized about it, but always from a lofty, almost detached place of perpetual peace. This is certainly something to aspire to, but it somehow makes his teachings feel a little more removed from the human experience. Philosopher Alan Watts put it another way, saying that if a person has truly transcended all negative emotions, then there is no longer a place for him or her on this planet.

As we drop deeper into the story of Jesus and his ministry, it becomes apparent that he is often intentionally vague when defining himself. For instance, when John the Baptist's own disciples ask him if he is the Messiah mentioned in Jewish lore, he does not give them a direct answer. Instead, he references the miracles he has done and the healings he has performed, leaving it to them to decide whether he is the Savior the Jews have been expecting for so long. What's more, when he curses the towns that have turned away from him, he makes it clear that it is not their refusal to worship him personally that will leave them floundering in the dark, but by ignoring the teachings and healings he has performed there.

Chapter Twelve

The Logic of Spirituality

One Sabbath day, Jesus and his disciples were walking through a field of ripe grain. As they were all hungry, the disciples pulled the heads off the wheat and munched on them while they walked.

Some nearby Jewish leaders saw this and were only too eager to hear what Jesus had to say about their behavior. "Your followers are breaking the rules of the Sabbath!" they said as they approached.

"Is that so?" Jesus replied. "Then what do you make of the story about David and his companions, when they entered a holy sanctuary and ate the bread that only priests were allowed to eat? And haven't you read how God forgives priests carrying out their temple duties on the Sabbath?

"What you are talking about is religious dogma, and what I'm talking about is true holiness. If you knew what the scripture, '*I prefer a flexible heart to an inflexible ritual,*' was really saying, you wouldn't be so hung up on your rules. As a child of God, I'm not a slave to the Sabbath, I'm in tune with its true meaning as a day of reverence and gratitude."

After speaking, Jesus made his way to a place where he and his disciples would often meet. When he arrived, he found a man with a crippled hand.

The priests saw this as another opportunity to trap Jesus, asking him, "Is it proper to heal someone on the Sabbath?"

Aware of their true intentions, Jesus replied, "Would anybody here not help an animal that had fallen in a ditch, just because it was the Sabbath? Of course not. So, why wouldn't you show that same compassion to a person?" After saying this, Jesus took hold of the man's hand and it was instantly healed.

Though they were furious, all the priests could do was slink away, vowing to ruin him sooner or later.

Jesus moved on, and though many people following him were healed, they were instructed to keep quiet about the miracles he performed. This was in line with a prophecy of Isaiah, which said,

"Look at the one who serves me so well. I love him so much and he is a delight. My spirit is alive in him! He will reveal me to the world, but he won't do it by coercion. His message will not be spread by fear or violence. He won't disregard people's feelings nor will he force his teachings upon them. Before long, his name will come to symbolize who I am and bring hope to everyone, even those who don't believe in me!"

Later, a blind and deaf man was presented to Jesus and was healed like all the rest. The people who witnessed this particular healing exclaimed, "This must be the Messiah we've been told would come!"

But the Jewish leaders were having none of it. "He's probably practicing black magic to do these things," they said.

Jesus quickly rebuked their slanderous words. "Let me ask you something; If a judge finds a person both innocent and guilty, has he not just cancelled out each verdict? And a family divided against itself does not last very long as a family, does it? By the same reasoning, how could evil use grace to tempt someone into darkness? If you're saying I employ evil to do good, you'd better be careful, for how else do you explain your own exorcisms?

"And once you come to the conclusion that evil is not healing these people, then it stands to reason that God must be here working through me in this moment.

"You need to know that here is a real spiritual battle going on, and you'd better decide which side you're on. There's no neutral ground here; you're either embracing God's laws of love and compassion or denying them. It's as simple as that.

"There's no wrong you can do on Earth that can't be forgiven, but if you keep rebuking God, then you are denying the very source of forgiveness and can never be redeemed. If you disregard my teachings, then that, too, is forgiven, as all things are in the Spiritual Realm. But hear me clearly; If you choose to keep denying God, He will honor that choice and you will be eternally separated from your Creator.

"Just as the fruit reveals how well the tree was tended, so do your acts reveal your true selves. An unpruned tree does not produce sweet fruit; just as a person who denies grace cannot commit acts of grace.

"You people have really twisted things around! What good are any of your words when they come from such poisoned minds? Don't you see that it's the quality of your heart, not some scholarly definition, that gives true meaning to your words? A genuinely good person, like a well-tended tree, produces goodness in both word and deed. But a person who has turned away from love is like a blight in the orchard. Make no mistake—every careless and hurtful word you say will come back to you in kind. Words are powerful, so use them with care. What you say can bring you closer to Spirit, or drive you further away."

Later in the day, a few religious scholars and priests came back to challenge him. "Teacher," they said, "we'd like to see your credentials. Can you produce some hard evidence that the one true God is behind all this? Why don't you perform some irrefutable miracle that will convince us?"

Jesus replied, "You seek a miracle, but your minds are so closed that you would not recognize a miracle if it happened right in front of you. I know that what you really want to see is some kind of magic trick, but the only proof you're going to get is the conundrum of non-proof, as with the transformation of Jonah. Like Jonah, who was in a fish's belly for three days, the transformed son will be in a grave for three days.

"The day to change your ways is at hand, and you would be wise to follow the Ninevites, who heeded Jonah's call to action. Now a far greater teacher is amongst you, but all you care about is superficial proof of my authority. Even the Queen of Sheba honored the teachings of Solomon, but you quibble about proof from one whose spiritual wisdom far surpasses Solomon's.

"When a man has rid himself of an unrighteous behavior, he is not in the clear yet, for if that place which held darkness is not soon filled with the light of holiness, he is extremely vulnerable indeed. In fact, if a man rids himself of one type of evil but doesn't quickly fill himself up with grace, many other ills could find a place to roost within him. Suddenly, this poor soul is worse off than when he only had one affliction! That's what you all are like: You think you've cleansed yourselves of sin, but if you continue to ignore God's message of love and compassion, you will be ripe for all kinds of evil to take up residence inside you."

While lecturing to the crowd, Jesus' mother and brothers arrived. They waited outside as someone announced their presence. "Just who do you think my real mother and brothers are?" he asked as he motioned to his disciples seated around him. "Look, here is my real family, for you all heed God's word. Don't you see that by accepting my teachings and joining me in my mission, you create a far more meaningful connection than the bonds of blood and heritage?"

Reflections

To hear Jesus use logic to explain his teachings is refreshing evidence that analytical thought and spiritual belief can coexist in the same conversation. Ancient scholars must have felt similarly, as the word *logic* comes from the Greek word "logos," which means "the Divine Word of God."

As Jesus addresses accusations being made by a group of Jewish scholars, he demonstrates that he is as adept at addressing pragmatic inquiry as he is at channeling the divine and performing miracles. Instead of dismissing their allegations from a position of spiritual authority, he skillfully employs rational thinking to deal with those who use thought and study as an entryway to God.

The conversation begins with questions about the Sabbath, the Saturday of each week set aside to honor God's Day of Rest after creating the heavens and Earth. The scholars believe they have set the perfect trap for Jesus, because he has obviously been "working" by plucking wheat and healing others on this particular Saturday.

Rather than directly addressing their accusations, Jesus offers a response in the form of a rhetorical question. Even if it was the Sabbath, would they themselves not save an animal that had fallen in a ditch? Knowing their answer would be yes, he then goes on to ask whether, by extension of the same logic, a similarly good deed should not be done for a person. As he builds his case, Jesus makes it clear that dogmatic religious practices should never interfere with our true spiritual mission of loving each other and serving those in need.

Later that day, Jesus restores the sight and hearing of a blind and deaf man, which stirs a crowd of onlookers to exclaim that he must indeed be the Messiah mentioned in their religious texts. Once again, however, Jewish scholars are quick to cast aspersions and go so far as to accuse Jesus of using black magic to perform these miraculous healings.

Jesus' thoughtful response to these new accusations is compelling, and it must have completely blindsided those making their claims against him. With authority, he reminds the scholars that anything working against itself is of course a threat to its own existence. As such, genuine acts of kindness are counterproductive to an agenda of evil, just as wicked deeds done in the name of compassion hinder the pursuit of leading a holy life.

As Jesus continues his scholarly debate, he lets it be known that every person must choose which side of the spiritual equation they are on, for trying to juggle an earthly life with a holy life is a conflicted and exhausting process that will not produce favorable results in either realm.

Towards the end of their conversation, the scholars who have been working hard to discredit Jesus have one last request. They ask for some kind of credential proving that God is the one responsible for the miracles he has performed. Jesus reads their intent and is easily able to fend off their veiled attack. To their point, he makes it clear that, if what they have already seen him do is not proof enough, then nothing will sway them.

This encounter makes me think of Saint Francis of Assisi. Though he never received any official credential as a Catholic priest, he proved himself to be a venerated authority through acts of service and love. First recited in the early 13th century in Italy, the prayer of Saint Francis is a beautiful invocation reminding us that the universal Laws of Spirit will always transcend the rules of any man-made religion:

"Lord, make me an instrument of Your peace.

Where there is hatred, let me sow love.

Where there is injury, pardon.

Where there is doubt, faith.

Where there is despair, hope.

Where there is darkness, light.

Where there is sadness, joy.

Oh, Divine Master, grant that I may not so much seek to be consoled, but to console.

To be understood as to understand.

To be loved as to love.

For it is in giving that we receive, in pardoning that we are pardoned. And it is in dying that we are born to eternal life."

CHAPTER THIRTEEN

Allegorical Teachings

Soon after, Jesus left the house and made his way to a nearby beach. In no time, a crowd had gathered, prompting him to head out in a small boat and use it as a pulpit. From the boat he addressed the congregation with allegorical stories.

"What do you think about this? A farmer is scattering seeds. Some of the seeds fall on the road and are quickly eaten by birds. Some fall into gravel, where they sprout, but because their roots do not go deep, they soon dry out. Some fall into the weeds, where they are strangled out by other growth. And some fall onto fertile soil, where they grow and produce a bountiful harvest.

"Are you getting what I'm trying to tell you?"

The disciples came forward and asked, "Why do you tell stories like this?"

Jesus replied, "Through your relationship with me, you've been given a first-hand experience, and thus true insight into how God works. Not everyone is going to get the same opportunity, so I tell stories to help prepare people for God's message. There needs to be a certain type of readiness within each of you for these messages to take hold, and that's what I'm trying to do—gently open people's hearts and minds. They can seek the answers to life all they want, but they're never going to find what they're looking for if God is not involved. I don't want Isaiah's observation to happen all over again:

"You listen but you can't hear anything. Your eyes are open but you can't see. You people are so stubborn!

"The truth finally comes, but then you block your ears and cover your eyes! You won't accept me, though it was me you invited to heal you.

"Similarly, all of you here are indeed seeing the actions and hearing the words of God through me right now. Many people, prophets and humble believers alike, would have done anything to be in your shoes.

"Think about the story of the farmer planting seeds: When someone hears but does not believe that the Holy Spirit is alive within them, this information remains on the surface and is easily lost. This is the seed scattered on the road.

"The seed in the gravel is the person who superficially gets excited about the message, but with no depth of soul or character, lets the words die out at the first sign of trouble.

"The seed cast in the weeds is the person who lets God's word grow amidst the mixed messages of fear, pride and greed, where it soon gets crowded out.

"The seed cast onto fertile soil is the person who already has a clear mind and pure heart who is able to be changed by God's Word and Love and act in accordance with it, producing a harvest more bountiful than can be imagined."

Then Jesus told another story. "Having Spirit alive within you is like a farmer who planted good seed in his field. That night, while his farmhands were asleep, an enemy of the farmer crept in and sowed thistles through the wheat, then slipped away before daybreak. Days later, when the wheat started to sprout, the thistles sprouted up as well. The farmhands came to the farmer and said, "That was clean seed you planted, wasn't it? Where did all these thistles come from?"

The farmer replied, "An enemy of mine must have done this."

"Should we weed out the thistles?"

"No, because if you weed them out, you'll end up pulling out a lot of the good wheat as well. Let them grow together until it's time to harvest. At that time, I'll instruct the harvesters to pull up the thistles and cast them out, then bundle up the wheat and store it in the barn."

"Another story goes: 'Having God within you is like a mustard seed that a farmer plants in the ground. Everyone knows that this is one of the smallest seeds there is, yet it produces a plant high enough for birds to roost within its branches.'

"And here's an old saying: 'God within you is like yeast that a baker works into the dough, allowing dozens of loaves of bread to rise.'"

All day long, Jesus told story after story like this, which would seem to confirm the following prophesy:

'I will open my mouth and tell stories. I will shed light upon that which has been hidden in darkness for so long.'

At the end of the day, Jesus dismissed the crowd and made his way back to the house, where his disciples asked, "What was the story about the thistles in the field about?"

Jesus explained, "The farmer who sows the pure seed is the messenger of God's grace. The seed represents God's word and the thistles represent people consumed by earthly pride and fear. The harvest is the coming end to this order of things and the farmhands are angels.

"The thistles being pulled up and discarded are those who have chosen to reject the ways of kindness and compassion. They'll complain of unfairness of course, but the deeds of their lives will speak much more clearly than their hollow words. At the same time, people who have embraced and shared love will forever exist in a state of love. Hear me on this; the life you choose to live here on Earth will greatly affect the life you will live in the Eternal Realm. God has never punished you for the choices you make, and He never will. Instead, He allows you to experience the *consequence* of your own choices, a process that starts here on Earth and continues in the afterlife.

"Are you understanding what I'm telling you?

"To discover that God is alive inside you is like finding a treasure that's been buried in the ground for years. How ecstatic would you be to stumble onto such a treasure?

"God Awareness is like being a jeweler on the hunt for pearls and who finds the most perfect specimen, then sells every other gem he owns to buy that pearl.

"Or it is like throwing a fishnet into the sea and knowing which fish are safe to eat and which should be thrown back. If you decide to take your chances and consume them all, don't complain about the injustice of what eating the bad fish has done to your health."

Jesus asked them directly, "Do you comprehend what I am saying?"

"Yes," they answered.

"Then you can see how every student of God's Word is like the owner of a general store, always knowing just what the customer needs, where to find it, and how to use it."

When Jesus finished speaking, he left for his hometown and gave a lecture in the meeting house there. Needless to say, people were amazed by his teachings.

"We had no idea he was this wise in the ways of the Lord!" they exclaimed, but in the next breath they were already starting to criticize him. "But isn't this Mary and the carpenter Joseph's son, who we've known since childhood? And don't all his brothers and sisters live around here, too? Who does he think he's fooling?"

To this Jesus answered wearily, "A prophet is taken for granted in his hometown and by his family." And because of their hostility towards him, he did not do many miracles there.

Reflections

This is the first sermon where Jesus liberally employs allegorical references to convey his ideas about God and Heaven. By the reaction of both the crowd and his apostles, it becomes clear that this way of preaching is unique.

I find it interesting that Jesus uses this method to convey many of his messages. Rather than arrogantly talking down to the crowd gathered around him, he invites them to participate in his teachings by placing themselves in the metaphorical scenarios he has created. In this case, he is allowing them to imagine that they are each the farmer in the field, which suddenly makes the lesson much more relatable and potent.

Joseph Campbell—a professor who travelled the world analyzing ancient religious teachings—came to realize the power of metaphor as a useful way to share complex ideas. In Jesus' day, Jews lived in fear of a jealous, angry, and wrathful God as described by the warrior-prophet Moses. Imagine how unique it must have been for them to hear uplifting stories about an unconditionally loving God from a humble and approachable rabbi.

To me, it makes perfect sense that Jesus would walk people through the way God and the universe work by speaking in parables. In much the same way, parents often read fables to teach children important concepts concerning morality, consequence and fairness. I remember my mother reading me a bedtime story about a grasshopper and a colony of ants. During the pleasant days of summer, the grasshopper played and danced while the industrious ants worked to stockpile supplies for the coming winter. When the cold winds began to blow, the unprepared grasshopper approached the ants, begging for food and shelter. The ants refused his pleas, reminding him that he should have been stocking up for winter while the weather was warm.

I never forgot this story, and, years later, a pastor brought to my attention that the fable of the grasshopper and the ants was actually inspired by the biblical account of Noah building an ark to prepare for a coming flood. I have no idea if there is any truth behind this interpretation, but it does serve as a reminder that allegorical stories can be powerful teaching tools, which Jesus masterfully proved many times over in his sermons.

There is much conjecture concerning the "missing years" of Jesus' life, which span nearly two decades following his family's return to Israel from Egypt when he was still a young boy. Many people believe that he either traveled to the Far East, or was at least exposed to the teachings of Eastern philosophers such as Confucius, Siddhartha Gautama (the Buddha) and Lao Tzu before returning home to Nazareth and beginning his own ministry. Although there is no historical evidence to support this theory, it does at least offer a plausible explanation for the striking similarity between many of Jesus' allegorical teachings and those of these Eastern mystics, all who lived many centuries before his birth.

In the end, how Jesus came to share his ministry through stories and parables will most likely never be known and, for me at least, is not all that important. What matters is that, through his unique approach to sharing spiritual insights, he became a conduit for connecting people to their loving Creator.

Chapter Fourteen

Grief and Faith

Around this time, Herod Antipas, the new ruler of the area and the son of King Herod, heard what was being said about Jesus. To his servants he confided, "This must be John the Baptist come back from the dead. That's why he's able to do these miracles!"

Months earlier, Herod Antipas had arrested John to placate his sister-in-law and lover Herodias' wishes, for John had called their intimate relationship adulterous. Herod had actually wanted to have John killed, but was afraid to issue the order because many people considered John a prophet.

But at a birthday celebration, Herod's and Herodias' desire for John's death was fulfilled. Herodias' daughter, a provocative dancer, had provided the entertainment for the evening. She was so good at her craft that, in a drunken state, Herod promised her anything she wanted. Having already been coached by her mother, the girl said, "Bring me the head of John on a platter." Unwilling to back out of a promise, Herod Antipas ordered John's execution and presented his head on a platter to the girl, who in turn gave it to her mother. Later, John's disciples retrieved the body for a proper burial and reported to Jesus what had happened.

When Jesus heard the news, he slipped away by boat to be alone and grieve. However, someone saw him leave and soon word of his whereabouts spread through the nearby villages. Once back on land, he was overcome by people suffering from numerous illnesses and he healed them of their illnesses and afflictions.

As evening descended, his disciples approached and said, "We're far from any town and it's getting late. Shouldn't you dismiss these people so they can go and find a place to eat dinner?"

Jesus replied, "They do not need to be dismissed to eat. Everything they require is right here."

"But all we have are five loaves of bread and two fish," they said.

"Bring what you have to me," Jesus instructed, then held up the food and gave thanks for it. After this, he distributed the bread and fish to the crowd, who were filled up with the offering. It is said that over five thousand people were fed and that there were even leftovers.

Soon after the meal was finished, Jesus told his disciples to get into the boat and head for the other side of the lake. After dismissing the crowd, he walked up a nearby mountain to be alone and pray and he stayed there until very late into the night.

Meanwhile, the boat transporting his disciples was far out onto the lake when a strong wind began to blow, battering the craft with storm-tossed waves. In the predawn hours, Jesus appeared to them, walking upon the surface on the water.

"It's a ghost!" they cried out in terror.

Jesus quickly set them at ease. "Take heart, my friends. It's me, and there's no need to be afraid."

Peter, emboldened by Jesus' words, replied, "Master, if it really is you, call me out onto the waves so that I may be with you."

"Come on, then," Jesus answered. "It is well within your ability to do so."

Startling everyone, Peter climbed out of the boat and actually began walking towards Jesus. But when he looked down at the churning waves and realized that what he was doing was impossible, he lost his nerve and was soon helplessly thrashing around in the water.

Jesus was there to save him. Reaching down and grabbing Peter's hand, he asked, "What happened to your faith?"

The two of them were soon back in the boat and the wind and waves diminished rapidly. Having witnessed all that had happened, the disciples were filled with awe. "You must truly be God's son to perform such a miracle!" they exclaimed excitedly.

Hearing of Jesus' return, more and more people began showing up at the lakeside to be healed, and many were restored to health just by touching his robe.

Reflections

The close relationship between Jesus and John the Baptist begins before they are even born. As the story goes, when cousins Mary and Elizabeth, (the mothers of Jesus and John) meet during the final months of their pregnancies, John leaps inside the womb upon hearing Mary speak of Jesus' impending birth.

Although there is no documentation describing Jesus' or John's relationship before meeting at the Jordan river, it is not hard to imagine that, if for no other reason than their familial connection, their bond is strong. Most tellingly, both men have strayed from the traditional teachings of Judaism and have been sharing very similar messages regarding the nature of the Kingdom of Heaven.

It is not hard to imagine how deeply Jesus is affected and saddened by the news of John's execution. We must not forget that, even to the most devout Christians, Jesus was as much a mortal man as he was God incarnate, so his human sense of loss and grief are not only understandable, they make him a more profoundly real and relatable figure to all who follow his teachings.

Later in the chapter, we drop into a moment when a great multitude of Jesus' followers are fed by nothing more than a few fish and loaves of bread. This event has taken on a life of its own over the centuries, often polarizing religious scholars, philosophers, historians and Christians alike. Are these events supposed to be taken literally, or is there a metaphor at work here? Could it be that the crowd is figuratively hungry for spiritual truth and, through Jesus' teachings, treated to an abundant feast of God's grace? Personally, the message that God's bounty is plentiful and that faith multiplies blessings is more important than debating over how a few scraps of food could feed thousands of people.

Finally, we come to one of Jesus' most memorable miracles, where he walks upon the rough and windswept waters of the lake to meet his disciples. This is obviously an incredible event, but what strikes me is the almost incidental acknowledgment that, for a brief moment, Peter is also able to walk upon the waves.

Peter's brief ability to perform this same miraculous feat is often overlooked in the retelling of this story, but it is a glaring omission in any discussion about Jesus and his ministry. Time and again throughout the gospels, Jesus informs his disciples and followers that they, too, are capable of performing the same type of miracles and healings he performs, if only they hold the faith and belief in their hearts that they are able to do so.

CHAPTER FIFTEEN

Religion and Spirituality

After word spread of Jesus' ministry by the lake, priests and scholars came from as far away as Jerusalem to see and, more often
than not, criticize him. They challenged him with accusations
like, "Why do you and your disciples not bother to follow God's
strict rules?"

But Jesus flung their accusations right back at them. "Are
you sure that you're talking about God's rules and not your own?
For God clearly says to respect your mother and father, but you
seem to think it's all right to cheat your parents out of what you
owe them and claim that the wealth will go to God instead. That
doesn't sound much like respecting your parents to me. The
truth is, you are all frauds, and Isaiah's prophecy describes your
actions perfectly.

"'These high-and-mighty people talk the right talk, but they don't bother to act in accordance with their own teachings. They put on a good show, but there is no substance behind it. What they're really doing is using God's name to push their personal beliefs and agendas onto others.'"

He then called out to those in attendance and said, "Listen closely to what I have to tell you: It's not what you swallow that pollutes your life, it's what you spew out."

Later that day his disciples came to him and told him how mad he had made the religious scholars and priests with his accusations.

Jesus just shrugged it off, saying, "Men are like trees; if they aren't planted deeply into the laws of Spirit, they will easily be uprooted by earthly temptation. They are blind men leading other blind men. How far can they go before they all lose their way?"

Peter said, "What do you mean by this?"

Jesus thought he had made himself clear. "Peter, are you trying to be ignorant? You know that everything you swallow just passes harmlessly through your intestines and back out again, right? It's the words coming *out* of your mouth and the deeds springing forth from your heart and mind that define you. Don't you see that a heart polluted by anger, murder, adultery, theft and lies is what causes harm to the people around you? A person may follow every ancient religious custom, but this does not cancel out their transgressions, and certainly it doesn't impress your Heavenly Father one bit."

From there Jesus and his disciples took a journey to Tyre and Sidon. They had only been there a few minutes when a non-Jewish Canaanite woman ran down from her home in the hills and begged, "Help me, master! My daughter has a terrible affliction."

Jesus did not seem to notice her, but when she wouldn't go away, his disciples pleaded with him to help her so that she would leave them alone.

Seemingly perturbed, Jesus replied that his mission was focused on helping the people of Israel, and that by helping her he would be depriving those more deserving. "It's not right to take bread from hungry children and give it to the dogs instead."

The woman thought of a quick response. "But don't the dogs begging at their master's table get a few of the leftover scraps?"

Jesus was impressed by the woman's quick thinking and faith, and said, "What you believe has already happened." Right then the woman's daughter was healed.

When they returned, Jesus made his way along the shore of Lake Galilee, then climbed a hill to prepare a place to receive visitors. Soon, people with all kinds of afflictions were being brought to his feet and he healed every one of them. When others in the crowd saw how the mute could now speak, the deaf could hear, the blind could see, and the lame could walk, they quickly spread the word that God was alive among them.

But Jesus wasn't finished yet. He called his disciples and said, "I feel for these people. For three days they've been here and now they have nothing to eat. I can't send them away with no food in their stomachs. They'd probably collapse on the way home."

"Are you saying you want to feed all these people?" his disciples asked. "Because there's no food to be found anywhere around here."

Jesus asked, "How much bread do you have?"

"Seven loaves," they replied, "and a few fish." Upon hearing this, Jesus instructed the people to sit down and prepare to eat as he gathered up the bread and fish. After giving thanks, he divided up the food and passed it out among them. Amazingly, over four thousand people not only ate their fill, but there were baskets of leftovers. After this, Jesus disbursed the crowd, then took a boat over to the coast of Magadan.

Reflections

For years, I co-hosted a popular weekly podcast, *Awakening Code Radio*. In some episodes, we interviewed prominent figures in the "New Age" or "New Thought" movement, terms often used to describe an ever-growing number of spiritual seekers who don't necessarily align with the teachings of any one religion. For years I was comfortable with the distinction between religion and spirituality, but eventually I began to feel like I was watching spirituality become just another religious expression caught in its own net; where wearing the right clothes, parroting the right buzzwords, even eating the right foods became more important than the heart-centered quest to connect with the very source of our existence.

In this chapter, Jesus addresses the same phenomenon. And while he is targeting the high-ranking officials in Judaism, it is easy to apply the same thinking to anyone who worries more about following religious dogmatism than doing the internal work required to enter the state of being Jesus calls the Kingdom of Heaven. To make his point clear, Jesus reminds his disciples that what someone consumes usually passes through them without much effect. Conversely, it is what a person brings forth from the core of their being—whether it be a thought, word or action—that reveals their true nature.

Peter has trouble comprehending the distinction between external and internal influence, and Jesus' exasperation reveals the depth of his struggle to share and make approachable his deep spiritual insights. He knows that Peter represents the compliant masses who, through no fault of their own, are unable to recognize that they have become more obedient to rules dictated to them by religious officials than to their unconditionally loving Creator. In essence, they have become the blind being led by the blind, a situation that can only lead to everyone becoming lost.

Later on, Jesus is approached by a gentile (non-Jewish) woman pleading for the health of her ill daughter. This is similar to the encounter he had with the Roman centurion, who asked for the healing of one of his servants. On that occasion, Jesus lauded the soldier for modeling what true faith looks like, but when the woman asks for a similar favor, she is met with an unexpected response of annoyance.

Reading deeper into this encounter reveals that Jesus is still on his journey of unlearning cultural prejudices, while at the same time expanding into the non-exclusive nature of God's love. In essence, he has momentarily become the student and the woman the teacher, for it is she that offers him a lesson through the metaphor of a dog deserving scraps from its owner's abundant table. You can almost hear the surprise and resulting humility in Jesus' voice as he is being reminded that he must live in accordance with the words he preaches to everyone else. This passage is often overlooked by Christian ministers, possibly because it depicts Jesus as an imperfect and judgmental prophet. But for me, it offers great comfort by revealing that he could suffer from temporary spiritual elitism just like anyone else. The true beauty in the encounter comes when Jesus, rather than rigidly holding the stance that gentiles are less deserving than Jews, acknowledges the important lesson he has learned from this woman and instantly decides to heal her daughter.

Many of us have heard the old Eastern proverb, "When the student is ready, the teacher will appear." These are wise words, made even wiser when we stop ourselves and ask, "In this moment, which one am I?"

CHAPTER SIXTEEN

Reading the Signs

Some of the same scholars and priests challenged Jesus again, pressing him to prove himself by showing them a sign from Heaven. To this he replied, "You have a saying that goes, *'Red at night, sailor's delight, red in the morn, sailors be warned.'* You think you're so shrewd in your ability to predict the weather; how is it that you can't read the signs of the times? People who are turned away from God always say they want to see some kind of miracle to prove His existence. Well, I'm here to tell you that the only sign you're going to see is the same sign Jonah saw." Then he turned and left them to ponder his words.

On their way to the other side of the lake, the disciples discovered that they didn't have much bread with them. To this Jesus remarked, "Watch out for the yeast of the Pharisees and Sadducees!"

Thinking that Jesus was scolding them for forgetting to bring enough bread, they whispered amongst themselves as to what they should do.

But he knew what they were saying and laid into them. "Why all this talk about not having enough bread? You baffle me with your lack of understanding! Have you already forgotten how all those people were fed when there didn't seem to be enough? Don't you see that the lack of bread to eat is not the issue here? What I'm talking about is the figurative yeast of religious dogma that enlarges itself like yeast giving rise to bread." Then it seemed like they were finally beginning to understand what he was talking about.

When Jesus arrived at the region of Caesarea Philippi, he asked his disciples, "What are people saying about me?"

They replied, "Some think you are John the Baptist reincarnated, some say Elijah, while others say Jeremiah or one of the other prophets."

Jesus pressed them further. "And what about you? Who do you think I am?"

Simon Peter replied, "You are our Savior. You have come to show us the ways of holiness, to teach us about the Kingdom of Heaven, and to spread the message that God loves everyone."

Jesus answered, "Bless you, Simon. Your answer didn't come out of a book or from the teachings of the elders. It was my Father who told you who I really am, and now I'm going to tell you who you really are. You are Peter, a rock. And on this rock will be built a church of such energy and power that nothing will ever be able to stop it!

"And that's not all. I want you to understand that, no matter what you've been taught in the past, there is no separation between Heaven and Earth. We live in a divinely connected universe where all things—thoughts, beliefs, words and actions—are interdependent and effect all other things. The idea that you are separated from anything or anyone is the greatest lie you have ever been told."

He swore the disciples to secrecy, making them promise not to tell anyone that, even though he was not the warrior king the Jews had been expecting to vanquish their enemies, he was indeed the Messiah foretold by their ancient prophecies.

Then Jesus explained to them that the time had come to go to Jerusalem and face the full wrath of the Jewish elders, which would probably result in his physical death.

Peter grabbed him and protested, "This can never happen!"

But Jesus was adamant. "Back away! Don't project your earthly fears and feelings onto the workings of Spirit. You do not understand the way your Heavenly Father operates."

Jesus approached the others. "Anyone who intends on going with me has to let me lead and must follow my example. Don't run away from hardship and suffering, embrace it. Just watch and I'll show you how. Through me you'll see that self-sacrifice is the only true way to finding out who you really are. Don't be like those who, by getting everything they could ever wish for, end up losing their spiritual selves in the process. Would you ever make that deal if you knew you were sacrificing your eternal soul just to have things go your way for a short time here on Earth?

"And don't worry about becoming rich businessmen, because in the Kingdom of Heaven, such wealth will get you nowhere. Trust me, the day will come when God's Spirit fully engulfs humanity, and you will all have more than you will ever need. This isn't mystical gibberish. This is real, and some of you standing here will be witnesses to this amazing transformation."

Reflections

I grew up in the yacht industry. During that time, it was not uncommon for me to hear boat captains recite the mariner's adage, *Red sky at night, sailor's delight. Red sky at morn, sailors be warned.*

This age-old quote is widely known amongst seafarers, yet most are unaware that the first written reference to it is attributed to Jesus himself!

At the beginning of this chapter, Jesus is once again facing his persecutors. I find it very telling that, while replying to their need to see some kind of miraculous sign from heaven, he reveals humanity's tendency to require an external affirmation when it comes to addressing the bigger questions about life. Some people seek out psychics or astrologers, and I'm sure most of us have had a moment of feeling lost and crying out to whoever may be listening, "Please, God, show me a sign!"

Yet if we feel deeper into Jesus' frustration with the Jewish scholars, it becomes clear that he is reminding everyone that we do not need to look outside of ourselves for any kind of sign that God is listening to us. God and the Kingdom of Heaven are always residing *within* us. In a rather cryptic response, Jesus says that the only sign his accusers will see is the sign of Jonah. You may remember the story of Jonah being swallowed by a whale for three days, which could very well be alluding to the fact that he himself will be interred for three days before being resurrected.

This exchange marks a pivotal point in the narrative of Jesus' ministry, where he begins to realize that he will very likely be charged, arrested and killed for his teachings. The irony of him facing a violent death for spreading a message of God's love is surely not lost on him, yet he explicitly states that he has no plan to back away from his life's mission of leading by example and spreading his spiritual insights for the betterment of humanity. From this moment on, we hear a certain urgency in his words and can almost feel him processing the awareness that he is living the final days of his earthly existence.

With his tone becoming ominous, he once again employs metaphor to communicate a deeper truth to his disciples. Gathering his students close, he tells them to beware the "yeast of the Sadducees and Pharisees," the wealthiest and most powerful Jewish officials. However, once again his disciples don't understand the reference, thinking he is talking about literal bread. Exasperated, Jesus clarifies the symbology of yeast in the process of making bread: even though it is just a small ingredient by volume, it has a major impact on the quantity, quality, taste and texture of the finished product. Figuratively, the yeast analogy is telling them that they need to be mindful of the purity of the ingredients they are incorporating into the recipe of their very being.

When he addresses his impending death, it is easy to understand his disciples' sense of dread and fear for him. You can almost hear a collective gasp as they are told the news, with Peter becoming especially distraught and pleading that this cannot be true. In the Bible, Jesus' actual response to Peter is, "Get behind me, Satan!" which illuminates his awareness that nothing can stand in the way of God's purpose for our lives.

Finally, Jesus provides them with some guiding principles concerning each of their ministries following his death. He reminds them not to get caught up in the quest for fleeting fame and wealth. Instead, they should focus on living a life of service and compassion, knowing their actions will be carried forward and multiplied in the eternal Kingdom of Heaven.

CHAPTER SEVENTEEN

Divinity in Everything

Six days later, three of the disciples got a glimpse of what Jesus was talking about. He had taken Peter and the brothers James and John to a high mountain. There, they witnessed something beyond their comprehension as they watched Jesus miraculously transform into a being of radiant light. A blinding brilliance poured out through his face, and even his clothes emitted a shimmering white light. As this was happening, they could feel the presence of Moses and Elijah in their midst.

Peter spoke excitedly, "Master, this is an incredible thing that is happening! To commemorate it, maybe I should build three shrines: one for you, one for Moses and one for Elijah."

While Peter rattled on about building the monuments, a luminous cloud began to form, and it quickly enveloped them. From deep inside the cloud, a voice announced, "This is my son, one who truly understands the boundless nature of my love for all things and all life. I delight in his awareness of my True Being. Listen to him and regard his words carefully."

Hearing this, the disciples trembled in fear. But Jesus made his way calmly over and touched each one of them saying, "Don't be afraid." When they finally found the courage to open their eyes, the cloud was gone and there was only Jesus standing there before them. As they made their way down the mountain, he implored them not to utter a word to anyone about what had happened. "When I finally prove that physical death has no hold over me, then you are free to talk about all that you have seen here today," he said.

Once back with the others, Jesus was peppered with all kinds of questions. "Why do the religious scholars say that Elijah must come first before the Messiah can appear?"

Jesus answered, "In a spiritual sense, Elijah, the one who was to prepare the way for the Messiah, has indeed already come, but none of the scholars recognized him. In fact, they treated him like a criminal, the same way they are treating me." When he said these words, they realized he was talking about John the Baptist.

At the bottom of the mountain, a large crowd had gathered. Among them was a man who approached Jesus, then fell down to his knees begging for a miracle. "Master, show mercy on my son. He's half out of his mind and suffers from seizures regularly. I brought him to your disciples, but they were unable to do anything for him."

Jesus was obviously frustrated by what he was hearing. "You are all still so disconnected from Source! How often will I have to repeat myself about the way Spirit works in your lives? Bring the child over here." Right then Jesus healed the boy.

Later, when the disciples had Jesus to themselves, they asked him, "Why couldn't we heal that man's son?"

"Because you are not accepting the full extent of what God can do through you to help others. To put it simply, if you were to acknowledge the holiness that is already dwelling within you,

you could tell a mountain to move and it would move. With true faith and acceptance of your divinity, there is nothing that can't be done."

As they regrouped in Galilee, Jesus said to them, "I am about to be betrayed, and the outcome will be my physical death. But do not worry, for this type of death will have no effect on my eternal soul, which I will prove to you three days after my execution." Still, the disciples were horrified hearing Jesus' speak of his own fate.

When they arrived in Capernaum, the local tax collectors came to Peter and asked, "Does your teacher pay the temple taxes?"

"Of course, he does," Peter replied.

But as soon as they were out of earshot of the taxmen, Jesus confronted Peter. "Answer me this: When a king levies taxes, who has to pay them, his children or his subjects?"

"His subjects," said Peter.

"Then the children get off free, right? But let's not kick up a hornet's nest if we don't have to. Go down to the lake and catch a fish. Within that fish will be a coin that will cover the taxes for both of us."

REFLECTIONS

There are many religious texts in the world that describe miracles performed by holy men and women. The Buddha is said to have been able to duplicate himself and manipulate the elements. Krishna was supposedly devoured by an enormous serpent but was able to inflate himself so large that he could not be swallowed. At 13 years old, Joan of Arc conversed with angels and led the French army to victory against the British. And, of course, the prophet Moses could call forth plagues and part the Red Sea.

So, what are we to believe about Jesus and the many miracles he performed? To be sure, his transfiguration into a being of pure light is an extremely challenging thing to contemplate. But, because I have personally experienced numerous miraculous healings and witnessed many things that defy human logic, I cannot discredit such fantastical accounts. Besides, my affinity for Jesus is not based on him being some kind of flamboyant magician, rather a fully actualized human exhibiting a sympathetic relationship with the forces of nature. He lives in an elevated state where he is not only able to comprehend the ways of God, he can also employ some of the same tools God uses to create miracles.

Upon returning from the mountain, Jesus and the three disciples accompanying him are met by a crowd of people seeking healing. In particular was a man begging for his son to be cured of seizures. The dismayed remainder of his disciples had tried to help the boy, but their efforts and prayers had proven to be ineffectual. When they gather around Jesus to ask why they were unable to perform the same type of healing as him, he does not say it is because he is more special than them, but because their faith is weak and they are not fully committed to the process. As he has stated many times in this gospel, Jesus reminds his proteges that they are just as capable as he is in regards to performing miracles.

This message is so important for us to remember, because it addresses the fundamental mechanics of manifestation. Rather than presenting himself as an anomaly, Jesus repeatedly makes it clear that we all have the ability to do extraordinary things if we see ourselves as extensions of Source Energy. We are not only connected to—but also have a direct impact upon—everything else. Once again, Jesus is alluding to his awareness of how the quantum universe operates, reminding us that we are all able to co-create with Source this experience we call life.

Chapter Eighteen

Love is Never Wrong

Shortly thereafter, the other disciples converged around Jesus and asked, "Who gets the highest ranking in God's Kingdom?"

Before he answered, Jesus called a small child over to sit amongst them. "Listen carefully, because if you don't get what I'm about to tell you, you will not only have no rank in the Kingdom, you will not even be eligible to enter! The simple truth is this; if you cannot become innocent like this child, then you may as well forget it. Whoever becomes simple again, free from all the trappings of this Earth, will find favor in God's Kingdom. The truth is, when you receive innocent ones like this child with the love of God in your heart, it's the same as receiving me directly into your soul.

"But if you instead take advantage of others' innocence, know that you have just invited ten times worse treatment into your own life. Seriously, you'd be better off if you were dropped in the middle of a lake with a rock around your neck. Woe be to those who take advantage of the pure at heart! There will always be the temptation to advance yourself by trampling others, but don't take that risk. The regret and grief you'd be inviting into your life would not be worth it.

"If there is an aspect of you that leads to temptation, you must consciously decide not to empower that particular aspect. You'd be better off without the use of some of your capabilities than to use them to commit sinful acts. For instance, if you've got a lustful eye, cast that lust from your life before it consumes you and affects your ability to see God.

"Be careful that you do not mistreat a single one of these child-like believers. You do realize, don't you, that each one of them has an angel that is constantly in communication with your Heavenly Father?

"Or consider it this way: If a shepherd loses one of his hundred sheep, doesn't he leave the other ninety-nine behind to find that one that is lost? And when he finds it, doesn't he lavish it with more affection and attention than the others? God in Heaven feels the same way. He does not want to lose a single innocent.

"If someone wrongs you, personally approach him and try to work things out together. If he sees your point, then you have made a friend. If not, keep trying until you have exhausted all reasonable effort. If that still doesn't work, then forgive him for what he has done, just as you would want to be forgiven when you do something wrong.

"Never forget that your action here on Earth initiates the same action in Heaven. As above, so below. As within, so without. The choices you make now are the choices you are projecting into the Eternal Realm and the words you say to each other are everlasting words. When two or more of you get together and pray or collaborate for something to happen, know that the whole universe is aligning to support your prayers and efforts! And when any of you gather together to remember me, I will be right there with you in spirit."

At this point Peter asked, "Master, how many times do I forgive someone who has wronged me? Seven?"

Jesus was taken aback. "Seven? Try seventy *times* seven! In other words, the right response never stops being the right response. Whenever you decide to withhold forgiveness, all you're really doing is exposing the personal boundaries you have placed on the infinite resource of love.

"The Law of Forgiveness works like this: There was a king who decided to settle all accounts with his servants. As it turned out, one of the servants had run up a high bill, which he could not even begin to pay. Accordingly, the king settled the debt by having the man's entire family put on the auction block to be sold as slaves.

"The distraught servant threw himself at the king's mercy and pleaded, 'Please give me a chance and I will do everything in my power to pay it all back!' Touched by the man's situation, the king decided right then and there to erase the entire debt and let the man and his family go free.

"But as soon as the servant was leaving the king's home, he encountered a friend who happened to owe him a small sum of money. He grabbed the man by the throat and demanded to be paid that instant.

"'I don't have it now,' the man explained. 'But I promise that, if you give me a chance, I'll do my best to pay it all back.' But the servant would not budge. He had the man arrested and thrown in jail until the debt was paid. The other servants were shocked by this act of cruelty, and they reported back to the king what had happened.

"In a rage, the king called the man back and said, 'You evil servant! I forgave your huge debt when you begged me for mercy. Shouldn't that have been example enough of how to treat someone who asks for the same kind of compassion?' The king was furious and mandated that the man pay back all the money he originally owed him. I'm telling you all this because that's exactly how it works in the Spiritual Realm. If you can't find it in your heart to forgive others, don't expect forgiveness for yourself."

REFLECTIONS

At this late stage of both his life and ministry, it's easy to imagine Jesus feeling less than confident in his disciples' ability to carry on in his footsteps. In many different ways, he has tried to share and model what it means to be a humble servant filled with grace and compassion, yet they appear to be fixated on such things as the hierarchical structure of Heaven.

As this particular conversation gets underway, Jesus is asked who ranks highest in the heavenly realm, as if they are in some kind of contest or race to see who finishes on top of a spiritual leaderboard.

In response, Jesus brings a young child over and lets them know that, unless they lose their competitive mindset and become as innocent as children, there will be no place for them at all. This may sound cruel and contrary to the idea of an unconditionally loving God, yet it is not. Instead, take a moment to consider the point that Jesus is trying to make when he proclaims that, above all else, innocence and purity of heart are what are required most to enter Kingdom of Heaven. If we are willing to trample over others to advance our status here on Earth, how can we possibly be prepared to transition into a realm of infinite love and compassion? As conscious human beings, we have the choice to be jaded or innocent, cruel or compassionate, but we must always realize that the choices we make create the reality in which we reside; whether here on Earth or the Eternal Realm.

The lesson continues when Peter asks Jesus about forgiveness, wondering how many times he should forgive someone who has done him wrong. To his mind, seven seems like a very fair number, while Jesus retorts that the number is closer to seventy *times* seven. In other words, if there is such a thing as right-action, it will always be right. The only limit to forgiveness is that which one person decides to withhold from another.

To make his point, Jesus tells the story of a king and his servant, each who have been placed in a position to either forgive or demand payment of a debt. As the fable unfolds, we can instantly feel the injustice metered out by the servant, but it is more than that: it is the halting of momentum of right-action. According to Isaac Newton's Law of Motion, energy moves until something stops it. In this story, the energy of forgiveness has been initiated by the king and would have continued as a radiant wave of forgiveness had the first servant not cancelled it out. Sadly, this servant, now faced with the consequence of his miserliness, is placed under arrest by the king who had shown him leniency earlier the same day.

As we move through these learning moments, we must decide whether we are going to employ the always-right responses of compassion and forgiveness, or if we are going to be the force that stops their momentum from reaching others. The choice—like any other—has always been ours to make, while the consequences of our choices have always been there to keep order in the cosmos.

CHAPTER NINETEEN

The Last Shall Be First

When Jesus finished with these lessons, he left Galilee and crossed the region of Judea on the other side of the Jordan River. Huge crowds followed him, and he healed them as he went along.

One day the Pharisees began challenging him, asking, "Is it legal for a man to divorce his wife for any reason?"

Jesus answered, "Haven't you read that God made man and woman as a complimentary pair? Because of this, a man leaves his family to be joined with a mate and the two of them become inseparable. And because this union is sacred, no one should take divorce lightly."

This answer didn't settle well with the Pharisees. "If that is so, then why did Moses give detailed instructions for divorce proceedings?"

Jesus was prepared for their tactics. "Moses' allowance of divorce was a concession that humans are capable of being closed-hearted and cruel. But to God, marriage is a sacred union based on love, so I shall make no such allowance. I'm telling you that if a man leaves his faithful wife and then marries another woman, he has committed adultery."

He continued, "Not everyone is cut out for marriage. Some people, from the day they are born, never even consider getting married. Others don't get asked or have their proposals accepted. And some don't get married for religious reasons. But if you feel deep in your heart that you have the capability and desire to grow into the wonder of a committed relationship, then do it."

Later, a group of children were brought to Jesus with the hope that he would bless them, but his disciples didn't want to be bothered and tried to shoo them off. Jesus, however, was happy to see them, saying, "Leave these children alone. Don't stop them from coming to see me, for God's Kingdom belongs to innocents like these." After blessing and laying his hands upon them, he left.

On another day, a man stopped Jesus and asked, "Teacher, what good deed must I do to ensure my eternal life?"

Jesus answered, "Why are you asking me a question that should be directed straight to your Creator? Do you not already know in your heart, the very place where God lives within you, what is good and what is not? It's really just as easy as doing what your heart guides you to do."

"Can you be more specific?"

Jesus replied, "Don't kill anyone. Don't commit adultery, don't steal, don't lie, honor your parents and love every person you meet as you would want to be loved."

The man replied, "I've followed all those rules, is that all?"

"Well," Jesus told him, "If you really want to know, go and sell all your earthly possessions. Give everything you own away to the poor. When you do this, all your wealth will be stored in Heaven."

This was the last thing the man expected to hear, and he was devastated by Jesus' words. He shuffled away dejectedly, for he had grown attached to the wealth and the things he had accumulated and could not bear the thought of letting it all go.

As they watched him leave, Jesus spoke to his disciples. "Do you see how hard it is for people who chase earthly wealth to live a spiritual life? I'm telling you, it would be easier to pass a camel through the eye of a needle than for a person obsessed with wealth to enter the Kingdom of Heaven."

The disciples were surprised to hear this. "Then who has any chance at all?" one of them asked.

"The truth is," Jesus replied, "nobody has a chance if they think they can do it all by themselves. But if you place your faith in your loving Creator, then you have every chance in the world."

Peter took this opportunity to jump into the conversation. "We left everything we owned to follow you. How will we be rewarded for that?"

Jesus acknowledged Peter's servitude. "Yes, you all have been devoted students and friends. When the two realms of Earth and Spirit converge and my teachings come to fruition, you will be right there beside me. And not just you, but anyone who has sacrificed the comforts of home and wealth will be rewarded a hundred times over. This is the great paradox: those who are last here on Earth will be first in God's Heavenly Realm."

REFLECTIONS

The more popular Jesus becomes, the more he is followed and harassed by Jewish priests and scholars. This time, their tactic is to see if they can get him to publicly renounce a law Moses had declared long ago regarding divorce.

Jesus does not shy away from their accusations, telling them that Moses' allowance for divorce is an acknowledgement of human frailty, not of God's design.

Later, a man approaches Jesus and asks him to clearly define the things he needs to do to enter the Kingdom of Heaven. By the tone of Jesus' response, it is apparent that the answer is not a mystery—think good thoughts, say good words, do good deeds. He invites the man to consider that the way to Heaven is not some complicated test, but a state of being which everyone can instantly access by acknowledging and acting upon their heart's guidance.

When the man asks if this is all he needs to do, Jesus tells him that the final step is to sell his possessions and give away all his money. He makes the point that the trappings of earthly wealth are often what distract people from their spiritual awakening, a materialistic condition more relevant today than it was 2,000 years ago.

When even his disciples question how anyone can ever enter the Kingdom, Jesus reminds them that it is all about priorities. The picture that comes to my mind is the old "Food Pyramid" diagram many will remember from grade school, where foods are arranged in ascending order according to their nutritional value. I can recall that whole grains and vegetables provided the foundational base of the pyramid, while sugar and processed foods occupied a much smaller space at the top.

In similar fashion, I can imagine an "Earthly-Life Pyramid," where toil and the pursuit of wealth sit at the base and command the most attention, while spiritual awareness occupies only a tiny percentage at the top. What Jesus was inviting his disciples to do was *invert* this pyramid and make their relationship with God the foundation of their lives and the accumulation of material wealth the smallest by percentage.

This upside-down way of looking at how we weigh our priorities leads Jesus to utter a mysterious phrase. In context of the conversation they've been having about wealth, he infers that those who willingly welcome poverty in exchange for communion with God, (in other words, those who have finished last in the race of Earthly success) will actually be the first arrivals into the Kingdom of Heaven.

CHAPTER TWENTY

Entitlement, Fairness & Gratitude

"Here is a story," Jesus began. "God's Kingdom works like this.

"An estate manager got up early one morning to hire the workers needed to tend to his vineyard. He found a few men in the town square and offered each of them a shekel—the going rate for a day's work—which they happily accepted. Later in the morning, he saw a few more men and told them he'd pay them each a fair wage to work in his vineyard for the rest of the day. These men also agreed. The manager went back to the square at noon, then again at 3:00, and finally picked up the last stragglers at 5:00. When the day's work was done, the manger instructed the foreman to pay the men, starting with the last hired and progressing on to the first.

"Those hired last were brought up and each given a shekel, leading those who had worked the entire day to believe that they would be receiving far more. But to their surprise, they were paid exactly the same as those who had only worked a few hours.

"Taking their pay reluctantly, they protested the seeming unfairness. 'My dear friends,' the manager replied, 'I do not feel that I have been unfair. Didn't you happily agree to the wage I offered? And what business is it of yours how I decide to pay anyone else? I find it odd that my generosity would make you feel that you have been cheated.'

"So here we have another example of how God works, where those who are last find themselves first in line for the rewards that He offers. You should all take heart in this story, for it shows that it is never too late to rearrange your priorities and accept the offer to live a life focused on spiritual growth."

Jesus, who was now on his journey to Jerusalem, gathered his disciples at the roadside and said, "Listen, we're almost there, and I have something to tell you. I'm about to be betrayed and handed over to the Jewish hierarchy, who will prosecute me and not be satisfied until they figure out a way to convict me. Then they'll turn me over to the Romans, who will torture and kill me. But as I've told you before, bodily death has no reign over my immortal soul. This will be proven to you three days after my execution."

It was around this time that the mother of the Zebedee brothers showed up with her two sons and knelt at his feet.

"What can I do for you?" Jesus asked her.

"Promise me that my two sons will receive the highest places of honor beside you in the Eternal Kingdom, one at your right hand and one at your left."

"My dear woman, you have no idea what it is you are asking me." Then he turned to the brothers and asked, "Are you willing to drink from the same cup as me?"

"We are," they replied.

Jesus' response was short and rather ambiguous. "As a matter of fact, you both will someday drink from my cup. But as to securing places of honor in the Kingdom, that is not up to me. My Father in Heaven has His own plans."

When the other disciples heard this, they became disgusted by the brothers' request for special treatment. Jesus saw that it was time to intervene and said, "You've seen how godless rulers lord power over people, right? This is not how it's going to be with you. Whoever wants to be great in the Kingdom must become like a servant. Whoever wishes to be first among you must be content to be your slave. And that is what I have done. I came to serve, not to be served. Finally, I will make the ultimate sacrifice, which will in turn save the lives of many."

As they were leaving Jericho, a large crowd followed them. Soon they came upon two blind men who were sitting on the side of the road. When the men became aware that it was Jesus passing by, they shouted out, "Master, please heal us!" The crowd tried to quiet the two men, but they just kept yelling louder to be healed.

Jesus came over to them and asked, "What is it that you want from me?"

"We want to see!" they shouted.

Moved deeply by their suffering, Jesus touched their eyes. Instantly their sight was restored, and they sprang up to join the crowd of people following him.

Reflections

The deeper we allow ourselves to drop into the inwardly-focused ministry of Jesus, the easier it is to imagine how Far Eastern spiritual teachings may have influenced him. As I have mentioned, his use of metaphor is unique for his day, and the lessons he shares exemplify radical compassion, humility, forgiveness, and service; uncommon topics for religious leaders of Israel 2,000 years ago.

The lesson of the estate manager hiring day laborers is timeless, as it reveals many great truths about our current notions of fairness and reward. Most of us can relate to this story through personal experience, where we are at first happy with a particular accomplishment or circumstance in our lives, only to feel this happiness fade through the process of comparison.

Jesus reminds us that our external notions of justice and compensation will often hinder our spiritual development. He asks us to quietly accept the "is-ness" of our reality, to sit in a neutral space of non-duality as we go about our lives. He invites us to step off the hamster wheel of competition and be grateful for what we *do* have, rather than focus our attention on what we feel we are lacking. In many different ways, Jesus keeps reminding us to direct our focus on ourselves and worry less about the status, wealth, fame or accomplishment of others.

As I consider this particular allegory, it's easy for me to recall similar events in my life. I mentioned earlier that I grew up in the marine industry, where I both sold and skippered yachts. I remember a particular boat show in Los Angeles, where I had the good fortune of taking a deposit on a large and expensive boat. I was thrilled thinking about how the commission from the sale would help clear out some old debt and even provide me some savings.

During that same show, a fellow salesman ended up selling a virtual fleet of custom-ordered boats to a charter company, a deal that made him a far larger commission than mine. I knew he had been struggling a bit financially, so I was happy for him and offered sincere congratulations. Yet, at the same time, I suddenly felt not only less exuberant about my own good fortune, but also a little jealous thinking that if the circumstances had been just slightly different, *I* would have been the one who made that sale.

The story about the estate manager and workers reminds us that, by placing ourselves in the downward-spiraling process of comparison and competition, we become our own distractors on the path of spiritual awakening. Time and again through the teachings of Jesus, we are reminded that Heaven is already here for us to experience on Earth, and that we ourselves are the only obstacles to experiencing this realm of abundance.

CHAPTER TWENTY-ONE

A Question of Authority

Nearing Jerusalem, the group arrived at a place known as Bethphage on the Mount of Olives. As they settled to rest there, Jesus sent two of his disciples ahead with these instructions: "Go to that village across the way. When you arrive, you'll find a donkey and her colt tethered together. Untie the donkey and bring them both to me. If anyone asks you what you're doing, tell them, 'The Master needs them' and you won't have any problems."

This is part of the whole story as it was told by prophecy.

"Tell the daughter of Zion, 'Look, your king is coming, ready to reign with grace, riding on a young donkey, the foal of a common pack animal.'"

The disciples went and did exactly as they were told. They led the jenny and her colt back to Bethphage, then laid their clothes on the jenny's back before Jesus mounted to ride. Nearly all of the people present threw their garments down on the road to give him a royal welcome. Others cut fronds from palm trees and threw them down as a welcome.

Crowds of people were all around him, shouting, "High praise to the son of David! Blessed is this man who comes to us in the name of God and Heaven!"

The whole city of Jerusalem had become aware of Jesus' arrival. All over town, people were asking, "What's going on here? Who is this man?"

The throng of followers answered, "This is the prophet Jesus, the one you've heard about from Nazareth in Galilee."

Once inside the city's gates, Jesus made his way straight to the Temple and threw out everyone doing business there. He knocked over the tables of moneychangers and upended merchant's carts, all the while angrily quoting scripture.

"My house is a holy place, but you have made it a gathering place for thieves!"

After the merchants and moneychangers had been cleared out, there was room for the blind and lame to enter. They came to be healed by Jesus, and they left the temple free of their afflictions.

Religious leaders were outraged when they saw all these things going on and heard the children running around shouting, "Glory, glory to David's son!"

Angrily they approached Jesus and asked him, "Do you hear what the children are saying?"

Jesus replied, "Yes, I hear them. Don't you remember in God's word where it says, *'From the mouths of children you have come to a place of strength and praise'?"* Tired and exasperated, he left Jerusalem and headed back to Bethphage for a good night's rest.

As they headed back to Jerusalem the following morning, Jesus and his disciples stopped at a fig tree to eat. But when they discovered it bore no fruit, Jesus became upset and said, "This tree shall never produce figs again!" At that moment, the tree shed all its leaves and withered before their eyes. The disciples stood there in shock, hardly believing that they had seen a healthy tree shrivel and die in an instant.

But Jesus was not surprised. He told them, "If you lead a truly spirit-filled life and never doubt your divinity, you'll perform much more impressive feats than this. For instance, if you tell this mountain to jump into that lake, it will do so. Everything, no matter how small or large, is affected by your genuine prayer."

Soon Jesus was back in the temple, teaching God's word to all who would listen.

The high priests came to him and commanded, "Show us some credentials. Who authorized you to preach here?"

"Before I answer that, let me ask you a question. Then, if you answer mine, I will be happy to answer yours. Regarding John's commission to baptize people: Who authorized it, God or mankind?"

The priests had been put on the spot. They huddled amongst themselves and whispered, "If we say 'God,' he'll then ask why we don't believe he's been given the same kind of authorization. But if we say, 'mankind,' we're in trouble with the people because they regard John as a genuine prophet." They decided to let the matter lie without further argument. "We don't want to answer that," they chimed in together.

"Then neither shall I answer your question."

Jesus continued on with his teachings. "Tell me what you think about this story. There was a man who had two sons. To the first one he said, 'Son, go out and work in the vineyard today.' The son answered, 'I don't feel like it,' but later changed his mind and did as his father requested.

"The father then gave the same instruction to his second son, who replied, 'I'll be happy to work in the field,' but then decided not to go after all.

"Which of the two sons did right by the father?

"The first one," the priests responded.

Jesus nodded in agreement. "You are right, and by the same reasoning I am telling you that the lowest members of society are more likely to enter the Kingdom of Heaven than you. John came and challenged you to change your ways, but you mocked his words. At the same time, the criminals and prostitutes who heard his message turned their lives around and were born again in Spirit. But even when you saw what was happening, you did not take John's message to heart.

"Here's another story for you to think about. There once was a wealthy farmer who planted a vineyard. He set the whole operation up, and then turned it over to his farmhands to manage while he went away on a trip. When it was time for harvest, he sent some servants to collect the profits from the farmhands.

"When the first servant got there, the farmhands beat him up. When the second servant arrived, they plotted together and killed him. The third one was pelted with rocks, but he managed to escape.

"Undaunted, the farmer kept sending more servants, and all of them were treated the same way. Finally, he decided to send his son, for surely the farmhands would respect his own flesh and blood.

"But when the farmhands got sight of the son, they were thrown into a rage of greed. 'Here comes the farmer's son! If we kill him, we'll have all this to ourselves!' And so they grabbed him, beat him, and killed him.

"Now, let me ask you this: What do you think the farmer will do to the farmhands when he arrives home from his trip?"

"He will kill them, and rightfully so," they shouted back. "Then he'll find other farmhands who will gladly pay him the profits at harvest time."

"That's right. It's even quoted in your scriptures:

'The stone the masons threw out is now the cornerstone.

'This was God's plan

'And we are in shock that we didn't recognize it!'

"That's exactly what's going on here. God's Kingdom will be taken back from you, you who He entrusted to care for it, and He will hand it over to those who will care for it the right way. If you can't see this, you're doomed."

When the religious leaders heard this story, they knew he was making a reference to them and they were enraged by the accusation. They wanted to have Jesus arrested right then and there, but he was already too popular with the people, most whom believed he was a genuine prophet of God.

REFLECTIONS

This chapter brings us to the beginning of the last week of Jesus' earthly life, when he rides into Jerusalem for Passover on a donkey and is greeted warmly by people waving palm fronds as he passes. Today, many Christians acknowledge this moment by attending Palm Sunday services the week before Easter.

Once he enters the city and makes his way to the temple to preach, he is angered by the commercial activity he sees taking place within its walls. In a fit of what some would call "holy rage," he overturns the tables and carts of moneychangers and merchants.

For some people, this anger reveals the relatable human essence of Jesus, but for others it serves as a precedent allowing spiritually-condoned acts of destruction and violence. To this day, many people cite this one example of him flipping over a few tables as justification to do far more horrible things to one another. For centuries, wars and acts of terrorism have been committed by Christians under the banner of "righteous violence," an oxymoron of the highest order. A person does not kill in the name of Jesus any more than they scream in the name of silence or drink alcohol in the name of sobriety.

While in Jerusalem, Jesus is once again badgered by Jewish priests who believe they can trick him into saying or doing something that could be used to persecute him. Most of their challenges are effortlessly tossed aside or turned back on them, but when they ask him about what credentials he has to preach in the temple, he offers them a fable of a man who asks his two sons to work in his vineyard.

At the end of the story, Jesus asks the scholars which son was the true servant of his father, the one who said he would comply but did nothing, or the one who spoke in defiance yet actually did the work?

They of course answer the question correctly, having no idea that Jesus is going to use the moral of this story against them. Here they are, pridefully wearing their finest robes and quoting scripture, yet not acting on God's order to humbly serve others. On the other hand, though Jesus is not wearing regal clothes or reciting ancient texts, the actions he takes prove he is the true servant of God and thus authorized to speak in the temple.

Today, we call this "walking the talk," and Jesus demonstrates how important it is to not just say good things, but to actually do good things. This is such a simple instruction—one that even a child can understand—yet many people struggle to follow it. In psychiatric terms, the phenomenon of knowing the right thing yet doing otherwise is called "cognitive dissonance," a term that succinctly describes the conflict between humanity's life-affirming idealism and often self-destructive behavior. Every new moment offers us the opportunity to align our actions with our higher awareness, and there is nothing stopping us from being the loving and supportive people we desire to be.

CHAPTER TWENTY-TWO

The Setting of Traps

Jesus continued on with his teaching and storytelling.

"Entering God's Kingdom," he began, "is like when a king throws a wedding banquet for his son, but none of the invited guests show up.

"Even after the king sends out another round of invitations letting everyone know that wonderful food and wine will be there, no one comes to the banquet. By this time, the king is furious, so he instructs his servants to go into town and invite anyone they see just to fill the palace. Finally, with the banquet in full swing, the king makes his entrance and surveys the guests. To his dismay, he finds a slovenly character amongst them and orders his servants to throw the man out.

"This is what is meant by, *'Many are invited, but only a few are worthy of staying,'*" Jesus clarified.

All along, the Pharisees had been plotting together and thought they had figured out a way to finally get Jesus to say something self-incriminating. They sent some of their students, along with a few of Herod Antipas' followers as witnesses, to ask, "Teacher, we know you to be an honest man who isn't swayed by public opinion, so we have a question for you. Should we have to pay taxes to Caesar or not?"

But Jesus was onto their scheme. He responded coolly, "Why are you playing games and trying to trap me? Listen, do any one of you have a coin?

After one of them produced a silver piece, Jesus held it up and asked, "Look at the engraving on this coin. Whose image and name are on it?"

"Caesar's," they answered.

"Then give to Caesar what is Caesar's and give to God what is God's, for the two are not even close to being the same thing."

The Pharisee priests were stumped, and they shuffled off shaking their heads.

That same day a group of Sadducees, who don't believe in resurrection or an afterlife, tried to trip him up with a question of their own.

They asked him, "Teacher, Moses said that if a man dies before he can father a child, then his brother is obligated to step up and marry the woman. Here's a case where there are seven brothers, all who died and in turn fulfilled their honorable duty. Here's our question. When the day comes that all of the brothers are resurrected, whose wife was she really, for they all had been married to her for a while?"

Jesus replied, "Your question is flawed on two counts. One, you do not have a clear understanding of your own laws. And two, you also don't seem to grasp how God works. In the infinite Realm of Spirit, earthly things like marriage contracts don't make a bit of difference one way or the other. In Heaven, we will all be like angels, connected to God with every fiber of our being. And regarding your speculation that the dead will not be raised, you are half right, because in fact it won't be the dead who are embraced eternally by God's love, it will be the living! Think hard on this, because what I'm talking about is a person's eternal soul, not his or her physical body."

Even though his answer did not sway his tormentors, it greatly impressed the rest of the crowd gathered there.

When the Pharisees heard how Jesus had gotten the best of the Sadducees, they gathered their combined forces for an all-out assault. One of their theological scholars spoke for the entire group, posing a question he hoped would stump Jesus.

"Teacher, which of God's commandments is the most important?"

Jesus replied, "Love God with everything you've got: your mind, your heart, and your soul. This would be first on the list. But there is another that is equally as important—Always treat others the same way you would want to be treated yourself. These two commandments are the very foundation of Spiritual Law."

As the Pharisees regrouped, Jesus caught them off guard by asking them his own question: "Tell me what you think about the Messiah. Whose son is he?"

"David's son," they answered in unison.

Jesus retorted, "Then how do you explain that David, in a moment of spiritual clarity, referred to the Messiah as his master? Do you not remember this passage?

"*God said to my Master, 'Sit here at my right hand, and you will have no more enemies to worry about.'*"

"Now, if David calls the messiah 'Master,' how could the Messiah at the same time be his son?"

This confounded them, because they'd never considered looking past the literal meaning of the scriptures they'd studied. Not wanting to risk losing face in these public debates, they quit asking Jesus any more questions.

REFLECTIONS

Once again, the local priests and scholars continue their tactical maneuvers to get Jesus to say something incriminating, yet at every turn he flips their accusations around and offers them a glimpse into the way God and the universe work.

Through the story of a king hosting a wedding banquet, he lets them know that, while everyone has an open invitation to Heaven, those not already living a compassionate life will be woefully unprepared to handle the transition. This is by no means unjust, for if we choose not to live in loving service to others here on Earth, how could we possibly be ready to enter a kingdom first and foremost defined by love?

When the priests question whether they should pay taxes or not, Jesus provides a short answer that invokes a much deeper meaning. Once he brings attention to Caesar's image on a coin, he suggests that they give to Caesar what belongs to Caesar and to God what belongs to God. This is a brief and concise way to say that, while we are expected to abide by the laws and customs of society, we are not to let this interfere with our spiritual lives.

None of us can deny the obligations and challenges related to modern living—earning money and adhering to societal traditions and laws—but it is up to each one of us to not let earthly demands impinge upon or, worse, take the place of our relationship with God. Stated simply, while we are each invited to live in this world, we are not to be *of* it.

There is another exchange that stands out to me, as it reveals much about the human condition. Like shrewd lawyers prosecuting a suspect, Jesus' accusers construct a convoluted scenario about a widowed woman and a succession of brothers who each become her husband for a time. To spring their trap, the priests then ask which one of them will actually be her husband upon the resurrection.

Jesus wastes no time in responding, informing them that Divine Law is simple and rarely as complicated or open to interpretation as human law. He lets them know that they have become so mired in their twisted beliefs and convictions that they have lost sight of the true laws of Spirit, a condition that has only gotten more extreme over the centuries.

This powerful chapter touches on one of the most important themes of Jesus' ministry; the dualistic nature of life. On one hand, he tells us that we are encouraged to fully immerse ourselves into this earthly experience; to marvel at nature, cherish our relationships, and even honor the customs and laws of society.

At the same time, however, he reminds us that we are all invited to explore our connection with God and contemplate the deeper purpose and meaning of our lives.

The ability to simultaneously navigate life both here on Earth and in the higher realms is the truest expression of "Christ-Consciousness," where we realize that everything we do in this 3-dimensional world matters in the 5th-dimensional (and beyond) matrix of creation. Jesus reminds us that we are spiritual beings having a temporary earthly experience, and that our conduct here affects the trajectory of our journey toward either an ever-expanding state of love and compassion, or an eternally collapsing vortex of fear and hatred. At the moment, we call these two etheric realms Heaven and hell, but to physicists and philosophers alike, these are just expressions of the polarized nature of all things. Expansion could not exist without contraction, just as the relative sensation of heat could not exist without the cold in which to compare it.

What makes us unique is that we can choose the vibrational field we inhabit—that of light and love or darkness and fear—a choice that impacts every moment of our eternal, multidimensional existence.

CHAPTER TWENTY-THREE

Pride Before the Fall

While still at the temple, Jesus turned his attention to his disciples.

"The Pharisees and other religious teachers to come may be competent teachers of God's law, but be careful that you do not start honoring them instead of God. They may talk with authority, but the only real way you can gauge their authenticity is by what they do.

"Instead of being open conduits of God's limitless love, they make themselves powerful by burdening you with strict rules to follow. They take pleasure watching you jump through hoops of ritualistic practice that have nothing to do with God. Their lives are like never-ending fashion shows, with ornate garments one day and even more fancy prayers spewing out of their mouths the next.

"They love to sit at the head of the table basking in their self-importance, receiving all kinds of impressive degrees and titles, soaking up public flattery like sponges.

"Don't allow this to happen to you. You all have a single teacher, and you are all in the same class. Don't place yourself in some religious hierarchy where others have power or control over you. Let God be your only authority. No one else should carry the title of Spiritual Father in your life, for you have only one Father and He is in Heaven. Don't listen to anyone's plea to take charge of your lives. There is only God's word, and that is the word I bring to you.

"Do you want to truly stand out in God's eyes? Then step down out of the spotlight, not into it, and become a servant. I'm telling you, if you place yourself upon a pedestal, you are just asking to get knocked down. But if you're content to just be yourself and make use of the gifts God gave you, your life will have all the meaning it's supposed to have."

Noticing a group of Jewish officials, Jesus became agitated as he continued. "I've had it up to here with you Pharisees and religious scholars! You're nothing but a bunch of power-hungry frauds blocking anyone who wants to lead a truly spiritual life. You're so hung up on personal influence and status that not only have you denied your own entry into God's Kingdom, you won't let anyone else in, either! You're hopeless! You go to the far ends of the Earth to convert someone, but all you're really converting them to is a mirror-image of yourselves!

"What arrogance and stupidity you possess! You say that if someone makes a promise with his fingers crossed it's a lie, but if someone makes a promise with their hand placed on scripture, then that's the truth. What idiocy! Is the leather binding of a holy book more special than the skin covering your hands?

"If you shake hands on a promise, that's meaningless, but if you raise your hand to God, it's serious. Are you joking? What difference does it make? A promise is a promise, your word is your bond, and God is always there holding you to account for what you say.

"And how is it that you can keep such meticulous records of every little transaction between you, but somehow the enormity of God's love and compassion slips by you completely unnoticed? There's nothing wrong with bookkeeping and note-taking, but if you're taking the wrong notes, what good are you to anyone?

"You're despicable! You polish your outsides until they shine brilliantly, while your insides rot and decay from lack of attention. Work on your insides first, then worry about the outside later."

Jesus' accusations went on at length. "Your fraudulent ways are why I have sent prophets and scholars, yet all you ever do is torture and kill them.

"But you cannot hide from the atrocities you've committed. Oh, Jerusalem, killer of the prophets bringing God's word to your city, how often I've yearned to embrace you, but you would not let me! And now you are a city without a soul, a spiritual ghost town. What else can I say? Only this—I will not be with you much longer, and when you see me next, you will finally recognize that I am delivering a message directly from your Heavenly Father."

REFLECTIONS

Maybe it's because he knows his time on Earth is coming to a close, or perhaps he is just exasperated by the failings of humanity, but at this stage of his life, Jesus is definitely becoming more forceful and accusatory as he addresses the Jewish elite.

And while he is directing his scorn toward the self-exalted priests and scholars of his day, I believe Jesus would shine the same light of accountability on certain current religious leaders. He makes it very clear that the pursuit of material wealth and fame is diametrically opposed to living a spiritual life, yet there are many Christian megachurch "prosperity" preachers who proudly accumulate exotic cars, private jets, yachts and mansions as affirmations of God's favor. I recall an old bumper sticker that said, "Jesus is coming soon, and boy is he pissed!" This is a humorous statement of course, but it is not hard to imagine Jesus being the most disappointed by the priests and pastors who flaunt their millions in his name.

The teachings in this chapter are applicable to all people, not just religious leaders. For instance, when Jesus talks of humility and honor, he could easily be addressing anyone that has ever puffed themselves up with an egoic need for attention. And when he says that a person must clean the inside of their vessel before worrying about the outside, he is talking directly to all of us. He urges everyone to be true to their word at all times, which will someday make the idea of swearing on a Bible or some other external gesture seem silly. Let your word be your word, be authentic, tell the truth and always be honest with your emotions.

What becomes clear is that Jesus upholds the same degree of accountability for everyone, no matter their status or role in life. We are all God's ambassadors here on Earth, each of us a minister capable of sharing important life-lessons with one another. When a pastor friend brought this concept up to me, I realized that everything we think, say or do can be considered a teaching moment. Through selfishness and violence, we model to others what *not* to be, while living a compassionate life of service may very well inspire similar acts of kindness and grace.

CHAPTER TWENTY-FOUR

Signs of the Times

Jesus and a few of his followers left the temple area. As they were walking away, he said, "Don't be too impressed. Whether or not you want to believe it, this whole temple will be a pile of rubble before long."

Later in the day, as they were sitting amongst the trees on the Mount of Olives, the disciples asked, "Tell us, when are all these things going to happen? What sign will we see telling us that the earthly realm is over and that the of Kingdom Heaven has arrived?"

Jesus said, "Beware of high-ranking people claiming to be saviors of the world, for under false pretense they will deceive many.

"When cataclysmic times of disease, famine or war spread all over the planet, stay calm, because change and disruption is part of the nature of life here on Earth. Humanity is destined to fight the same wars over and over again, and there have always been diseases and earthquakes. But these are nothing compared to the true end of this age.

"It's going to be a very challenging time, and people will persecute and kill you just because you call yourself a follower of mine. From there it will get even worse, and it will be every man for himself.

"In all this confusion, a few charismatic and self-righteous charlatans will come out of the woodwork, promising safety and security. For others, greed will consume them and all they will care about is profit and control over their fellow man.

"In these unstable times, it will be crucial that you remain grounded in your principles of peace, compassion and forgiveness, so never forget to keep the flame of love burning inside you. You won't be sorry, and you'll be rewarded with an incredible life in the eternal Kingdom of Heaven. During the cataclysm to come, the lessons I'm sharing with you now will be received in a whole new way, giving humanity one last chance to be redeemed from the atrocities it has committed against itself. There will be a messenger of my teachings in every nation, reminding people that love is the only thing that will save humanity. Then, finally, this system that runs on fear, greed and control will be over.

"Be prepared when you see the ultimate desecration and ruin of Jerusalem's Temple. If you've read what the prophet Daniel had to say about this, you know what I'm talking about. If you're living in Judea at the time, get out fast. If you're working in the yard, don't even go back to the house to get anything. This will be an especially tough moment for pregnant women and nursing mothers. Pray it doesn't happen during the winter or on a Sabbath.

"This will truly be a difficult transition, one like the world has never seen. In fact, if these dire times continued for long, no one could survive them. But on account of God's love for His children, the extreme suffering will be cut short.

"If anyone announces, 'Here comes the one who will rescue us,' don't fall for it. False prophets and dishonest officials, with their impressive credentials and flashy performances, will fool many people who should know better. But, remember, I gave you fair warning.

"If someone gets all excited and shouts that your savior is out in the country, or downtown, or speaking in a particular church, don't even bother acknowledging them. When the time comes and Spirit is fully revealed, it will happen to everyone, everywhere, all at the same time. You should ignore the crowds gathering at one place or another, because that's not how it will be.

"There will be no mistaking the signs that a new order is taking hold, for it will seem like everything you thought you knew is being turned completely upside down. Day will be like night, deceit will be proclaimed as truth, and chaos will rule over the land!

"Then it will happen—a spiritual transformation like nothing you can imagine. You will finally be able to see me in my celestial form and glory, because you will be in yours. But the people who have denied their loving Father all their lives will suddenly have to confront Him and, sadly, they won't be ready. They'll watch with awe and disbelief as this new age begins, bringing those who are spiritually awake together under God's grace and love.

"Take a lesson from the fig tree. When you see the first green buds on its branches, you know that spring will be coming soon, and that's how it will be. When you see the signs I've described, you'll know the old order is coming to a close and the new one is just around the corner. And don't assume I'm talking about some distant event that has nothing to do with you. I'm talking about an era that you are all a part of, a moment that includes every person standing here today.

"But no one knows the exact date and time of this amazing transformation—not the angels, not even me. Only the Creator knows.

"The new era will arrive like that famous flood in Noah's day. Before the rains came, everyone was going on with their busy lives, not noticing anything until it was too late. They were caught completely off guard by the flooding, swept away before they even knew what was happening.

"This new spiritual dimension will be like that. Two men will be working in the field—one who has lived a spiritual life, the other an earthly life—and the one with love in his heart will be swept up in this dynamic shift while the other is left behind. Or two women at work, one whose soul is prepared to ascend and the other barely able to comprehend that a dramatic shift is even taking place. I am telling you to stay alert and aware, because no one knows the exact timing. Is a person better prepared if he knows a burglar is planning to break into his house? Of course, and that's how vigilant you should be, because God is indeed planning a loving assault on your heart.

"Who here would consider themselves good management material? I'm talking about someone who is always on task and looking out for the benefit of others, because that's the only way to live if you want to see God's plan more fully revealed.

"But if you are a person who has ignored the laws of love and compassion, how could you possibly be ready to graduate to an even higher level of consciousness? No, as your reward, you will get more of that which you have chosen for yourself here on Earth."

Reflections

Regarding the many apocalyptic references found in the Bible, the most familiar quotes come from the Book of Revelation, which was written by the apostle John somewhere around the year AD 95. Many people have heard or read bits and pieces of this book, which is full of mysterious apparitions and nightmarish images climaxing in a final battle between the forces of good and evil. Some people take John's prophecies literally, noting that there are historical aspects to his predictions. One such prophecy has the climactic battle taking place on the Palestinian plane of Megiddo, the geographic and cultural inspiration for the term *Armegeddon*.

In ancient Greek, *Apocalypse* means "to pull the lid off something." In context to John's dire visions, it signifies a future moment in time when all will be revealed. Will this dramatic moment be heralded by four ghostly horsemen riding across the sky? Will people be coerced into receiving "the mark of the beast" in order to function in society? Will there be an evil antichrist leading the battle against Jesus and the forces of good? These are just a few of the predictions John made regarding this tumultuous time, and hundreds of books have been written trying to dissect and clarify their true meaning.

I often wonder why the most familiar apocalyptic references come from John's revelations, when Jesus himself talks at length about this dramatic moment. To me, his predictions regarding the end times are far more relatable, making it easy to draw parallels to certain current events. He foresees a time of global confusion and chaos, when the very foundation of what we call reality will unravel. The masses will frantically herald certain individuals as heroes and saviors, only to later recognize them as charlatans and profiteers preying on society's fears. War, disease and famine will spread over the entire planet to a degree never seen before, and there will be great dissent between citizens and their official leaders. He also alludes to a world-wide system of delivering news and information, when everyone on the planet will be subjected to reports about what action should or should not be taken to survive this global upheaval.

As Jesus describes the coming apocalypse, it's as if he is aware of some of the more intriguing aspects of physics that would not be known for nearly 2,000 years. For instance, it was less than a century ago when German physicist Erwin Schrodinger realized that multiple realities can exist in any given moment. In his classic thought experiment, there is a cat locked in a box which contains poisoned food. He realizes that all conjecture regarding whether the animal has eaten the food and died or is still alive can only be proven by removing the lid and peering into the box. Until then, the cat must be considered both dead *and* alive at the same time. This may sound strange to most of us, but the "Schroedinger's Cat" conundrum became an important milestone in the pursuit of understanding how the quantum universe works at all levels.

To the point, Jesus describes a future event when some people on Earth will be instantly propelled into a higher state of consciousness, while others will be frantically hoping for a return to life as they have known it. He shares a vision of two people working in a field, where one person is swept up in a rising flood of spiritual awareness, while the other is left behind wondering what is going on. This clearly implies that both are still alive, but are now somehow occupying space in two completely different realities.

As I see it, this is already happening. On one side of the equation, there is a large percentage of the world's population that is willfully relinquishing freedoms and agreeing to be monitored and manipulated by large corporations, charismatic billionaires and oppressive governments.

At the same time, there are people who are taking a step back and realizing that something is not right. They see and feel at a gut level that the process of our organic ascension is being squelched by an elite few who—through technology and dominion over money and resources— want to keep us distracted, complacent, and controlled. Those in power *need* us to stay "left behind" in this fear-based reality to serve as their subordinate laborers, consumers, soldiers and taxpayers.

Like Schroedinger's Cat, we must consider that humanity is both awakening to our greater potential and moving toward collapse at the same time, with the choices we make here on Earth being the deciding factor. Someday, the proverbial lid will be removed and we will each experience a personal revelation as to which side of the equation we were on.

While Jesus states that no one, not even him, knows the exact time the final act of this great transition will occur, his words regarding the preemptive events leading up to it seem highly relevant to this particular time in history. And if this is true, what should we do to prepare ourselves for this momentous shift? Where should we go when things get really unstable?

We should do what Jesus tells us to do on any other day—love one another. And we should go where he has always told us to go—within. The instructions he has given us can be applied at any time, to any circumstance, on any scale. Live your life guided by love, be of service, and do unto others as you would have them do unto you. No world event, not even an apocalypse, changes Jesus' message regarding what will save our species and provide us entry into the higher dimensional realm we call Heaven.

CHAPTER TWENTY-FIVE

The Flock of Sheep and Goats

"The end of this era will be like ten young women who were waiting for the groom to show up at his reception, because that's when the lavish wedding banquet begins. Five of them were prepared with full lamps and a supply of extra oil, while the other five believed that the oil in their lamps would be enough. One night, when it was announced that the bridegroom was coming, they all went out with their lamps blazing to welcome him. However, his arrival was taking longer than everyone expected and the unprepared women were soon out of fuel.

"'Share some of your oil with us,' they pleaded.

"'Not a chance. Go and buy some more for yourselves.'

"Unfortunately, while they were gone, the bridegroom showed up, the festivities began, and upon their return the unprepared women found themselves locked out of the banquet hall. When they pounded on the door, the groom came out and said, 'I'm sorry, but I don't know you,' and then locked them out for good.

"I am asking you to not be like those women. Always be ready for the end of this order, because what follows will be more incredible than you can possibly imagine.

"Here's a story of a property owner who gave each of his servants a generous sum of money to manage while he was away on a trip. When he returned, he discovered that most of them had invested the money wisely and had more waiting for him than when he left.

"These men were rewarded with better positions of employment. However, in the name of safety, one of the servants hid his masters' money under the bed and had only the original amount to give back.

"The property owner was furious. 'Don't you know that any worthwhile reward will require taking a risk? And since you knew I was expecting the best, why would you do less than the least? After all, you could have deposited it in a savings account and made a little interest!' With that, the property owner took the money back, gave it to the servant who'd made the most profit, and fired the other one on the spot. Do you see that I'm telling you how important it is to invest in your spiritual growth?

"There will be a time when you and everyone who has ever lived will get the chance to meet me in the Heavenly Realm. You will be like a giant flock of sheep and goats combined that is being sorted by their shepherd, with the goats going to the left and the sheep to the right. Then I will say to the sheep, 'Come and receive the bounty that's been waiting for you since time began. This is your reward because,

I was hungry and you fed me,

I was thirsty and you gave me a drink,

I was homeless and you provided me with shelter, I was cold and you gave me warm clothes,

I was sick and you cared for me,

I was in prison and you came to visit.'

"Then you will say, 'Master, we don't understand. We never saw you hungry, or thirsty, or sick or any of those other things.'

"To that, I will reply, 'Hear me clearly. Whenever you showed grace and compassion to those less fortunate, it was as if you were caring directly for me. And indeed, you were, because we are all eternally connected to each other—the holy and unholy, the wretched and the mighty alike.'

"After this, I will turn to the goats on the left and say, 'What are you doing here? You don't belong. You chose to live your life on Earth denying love and grace, a choice the universe has always honored and, unfortunately for you, always will. This is because,

I was hungry and you withheld food,

I was thirsty and you gave me nothing to drink, I was homeless and you looked away,

I was cold and you couldn't have cared less, I was sick and you didn't tend to me,

I was in prison and you ignored me.'

"To this, you are going to say, 'What are you talking about? When did we ever deny you mercy or grace when you were in need?'

"My reply will not be easy to swallow, for this is how it works. Whenever you turn away from anyone in need, it's the same as if you are turning directly away from me. Don't you see that I live in everyone, including you, just as you live in everyone, including me? And since this is so, I am present not only in those who have easy lives, but in the unfortunate as well.'

"Then the goats will be turned away, free to eternally roam the barren landscape they have created for themselves."

Reflections

As a way to educate his disciples and followers, Jesus once again employs metaphor to describe the coming new era. He compares this momentous event to a grand wedding reception, where ten women—some more prepared than others— are waiting to meet the groom with an oil lamp lit in his honor.

The obvious moral of this story is that everyone must be similarly prepared for the dawn of a new paradigm on Earth, and Jesus' eternal words have provided us with an action plan to be ready for it.

The advice he is giving his disciples is the same advice he would give anyone today. Love and support one another. Stay humble. Forgive without limit. If a person does these things, they will not only be ready for the dawn of a new age of enlightenment, they will actually be expediting its arrival.

In the next lesson, Jesus describes a wealthy property owner who leaves a sizeable sum of money with each of his servants to manage while he is away. Upon his return, he learns that one of the servants hid his portion under a bed for safekeeping. The property owner admonishes the servant, saying that risk is often involved to achieve reward.

While the story of the bridegroom focuses on the need for preparedness, the analogy of the property owner highlights the importance of investing. When we think of the word "investment," we usually think in terms of money, but Jesus is inviting us to look deeper into its meaning. Since he is talking about the requirements needed to continue our journey into the now-and-forever Kingdom of Heaven, what we must invest in most is *ourselves*. Thematically, this inward-focused analogy resonates with so many of Jesus' other teachings, where he affirms that everything we need to live in the Kingdom of Heaven is already inside of us. We just need to make sure that the investments we've made in our spiritual growth are not stagnating or losing value.

As I've mentioned, *entanglement* is a term used in quantum physics to explain the connectedness of all things to all other things. Once again, Jesus reveals his awareness of this concept when he explains to his disciples what it will be like in the final days of the old order. With knowing conviction, he tells them he will be guarding the gates of Heaven, ready to separate the sheep from the goats. When he says that he will allow entrance to anyone that has ever shown him mercy and acts of kindness, he is well aware that most people will have never personally interacted with him. But if everything and everyone in the entire universe is intimately entangled, then how they have treated each other is—by extension—how they have treated him.

Likewise, when he states that he will decline entrance to people who have treated him cruelly, the same analogy applies. The lesson may seem harsh, but it is just another way of saying that, while we are free to choose our actions, we are not free of the consequences of those actions. In physics, the word *causality* is used to explain that any physical thing or situation that has ever existed happened through causation. In that regard, we cannot expect cruelty to be the cause of our admission to Heaven any more than we can expect harmful addictions to be the cause of health or war the cause of peace.

I have a friend who traveled to India many years ago and had the opportunity to meet Mother Teresa at an orphanage. When she asked him if he would like to meet Jesus, he was caught off guard, but of course said yes. Without another word she took his hand and led him outside toward a ragged and filthy man begging in the street. When the two men's eyes met, she gave my friend a knowing nod, then quietly removed herself from their company. I have never forgotten this story, as it brings to life the message that we should treat everyone the same way we would treat Jesus himself. This is how we choose whether we are part of the flock of sheep or goats.

CHAPTER TWENTY-SIX

The Final Hours

After Jesus finished speaking about the end times, he told his disciples, "As you know, Passover is in two days. That's when I will be betrayed and handed over to the Romans to be put to death."

Already, some religious leaders were meeting in the chief priest's chambers, plotting the most covert way to seize and kill Jesus. They agreed that it should not be done during Passover, as this would probably start a riot.

When Jesus and his disciples were at Bethany as guests of Simon the Leper, a woman approached and anointed Jesus with an expensive bottle of perfume.

When the disciples saw this, they angrily scorned her. "What a waste! She could have sold that perfume and given the money to the needy."

Jesus stopped them. "Why are you judging this woman? She has just done something profoundly significant for me. Don't you see that the poor will always be with you, but I will only be here for a short while longer? When she poured the perfume on my body, what she really was doing was anointing me for burial. You can be sure that, just as my teachings will live on, so will the actions of this woman be remembered."

Around this time, Judas Iscariot, who was one of the twelve disciples, went to the high priests and asked, "How much will you pay me if I tell you where Jesus is staying?" They talked it over amongst themselves and offered thirty pieces of silver, which Judas accepted and began to plot his treacherous act.

On the first of the days of yeast-free bread, the disciples came to Jesus and asked, "Where shall we prepare the Passover meal?"

Jesus replied, "Go into the city, find a certain man I know and tell him, 'The Teacher says that his time has come and is asking to celebrate Passover at your house.'"

The disciples followed these instructions, and there they prepared the Passover meal.

After sunset, as Jesus and the disciples were sitting around the table, he told them, "This is a difficult thing to say, but someone you all know is going to hand me over to the conspirators plotting to kill me."

They were shocked by Jesus' words, each wondering in horror, "It isn't me, is it?"

Jesus answered, "The one who will do this is someone I eat with daily and who passes me food at the table. In one way, it will be done so that the scriptures can be fulfilled, but that's a small consolation for anyone who would commit such an act. No, it would be better to never have been born than to betray me."

That's when Judas, who had already done the deed, piped in, "It isn't me, is it?"

"Don't play me for a fool, Judas," Jesus replied.

During the meal, Jesus took and blessed the bread, broke it, and gave a piece to each disciple, saying, "Take this bread, and let it be a symbolic reminder that I willingly gave up my earthly body for you."

Then, taking a cup of wine he added, "And regard this wine as blood poured out, just as God's forgiveness pours out for all who accept it."

After they drank, Jesus added, "I won't be celebrating with you like this until we are joined together again in the Heavenly Realm."

When they were done, they sang a hymn and went back to the Mount of Olives for the night. As they were settling in, Jesus told his disciples, "Be warned, the events that are about to take place tonight are going to scatter you all in a frenzied panic, running around like a bunch of lost sheep. This will fulfill the scripture that says, *'The shepherd will be struck down, and the sheep will scatter.'* But know that my spirit will not be dead, and you will feel me leading you to Galilee."

Peter spoke up, "Master, even if everyone else turns and runs, I promise you I will not."

"I know you want to believe that, Peter, but the truth is this. Before the rooster crows tomorrow morning, you will have denied me three times."

Peter shot back, "Even if I had to die right alongside you, I would never deny you!" After he said this, all the disciples expressed the same sentiment.

After dinner, Jesus led them out to the Garden of Gethsemane and said, "Stay here while I go and pray awhile." Taking along Peter and the two sons of Zebedee, Jesus broke down and admitted, "My heart is heavy knowing what's going to happen to me. Please, stay here and comfort me in my time of need."

Walking a little further ahead of them, Jesus fell down to the ground and wailed, "Father! Does it really have to happen like this? Isn't there any other way? I feel there is so much more for me to do, but I would never ask that anything be done according to my will, only to Yours."

When he came back to where he left Peter and the two brothers, he found them sound asleep. Waking Peter, he asked, "Here I am preparing for my death, and you can't even stay awake a few hours to comfort me? This is a critical moment to be alert and in prayer, or you will be led into temptation without even knowing you're in danger. There is a part of you that is so awake, but there's another part of you that is as weak and lazy as an old dog sleeping by the fire."

After saying this, he left them once again to be alone and pleaded, "Father, if there is no other way than this, then I accept it fully. I am ready for Your will to be done."

Jesus checked back in on the three disciples. Finding them fast asleep once again, he went away to pray one last time. Upon his return he asked, "Are you going to sleep here all night? Look! My time is up, here come my betrayer and the men who will prosecute me."

He hadn't finished speaking when Judas showed up with a group of religious leaders and priests, some carrying swords and clubs. Judas had worked out a signal to them, saying, "I'll kiss the one you're looking for." According to the plan, Judas went straight to Jesus and greeted him with a kiss.

Of course, Jesus knew what was going on. "Why the charade, Judas?"

Just then the priests grabbed him. In the scuffle, one of Jesus' disciples pulled out a sword and sliced the ear off of one of the priest's servants.

Jesus ordered him to stop. "Put your sword away! Haven't you learned anything from me? Those who live by violence are doomed to die by violence. Don't you know that I could call on God right now and He would send an army of angels to protect me? But if I did that, how would the scriptures be fulfilled?" He then turned back and addressed the mob. "What's the meaning of coming after me in the dark and pouncing on me like I was some dangerous criminal? I've been in the temple every day teaching right out in the open and you've never laid a finger on me. No, you've done it this way so that the prophetic scriptures would be fulfilled."

Fearing for their lives, the three disciples ran away from the attackers.

The group that seized Jesus led him to the Chief Priest Caiaphas' house, the place where the leaders and scholars had been plotting Jesus' abduction. Peter had followed them at a safe distance until they got to the priest's courtyard, where he slipped in and mingled inconspicuously with the servants.

The high priests, along with the Jewish Council, had come up with a list of charges they believed would lead to Jesus' execution. But as they stepped up to make their claims, each one was refuted for one reason or another.

Eventually, two men came forward and testified that Jesus had said, "I can tear down this temple of God and rebuild it in three days."

The Chief Priest shot up and said, "What do you have to say to this accusation?"

Jesus did not respond.

Angrily, the priest demanded, "Under the authority of Yahweh, tell me if you are the Messiah we have been waiting for, the Son of God."

Jesus was direct. "You yourself have said it, and soon enough you will see it with your own eyes. 'The Savior, seated at the right hand of the Mighty One, arriving on the clouds of Heaven.'"

Hearing this, the Chief Priest became furious, tearing at his robes. "Blasphemer! You all heard it! We don't even need witnesses to bring charges against him! Are you going to stand for any more of this?"

In a frenzy, they started yelling, "Death! His blasphemy has sealed his own death sentence!"

Then they began spitting in his face and pushing him around. They jeered and slapped him, taunting, "Come on and give us a prophecy, Messiah. Who hit you that time?"

Meanwhile, Peter was sitting out in the courtyard, hoping to get some information as to what was going on. As he sat there, a servant girl approached him and said, "I know you. You were with Jesus from Galilee."

In front of everyone, Peter snapped back, "I have no idea what you are talking about."

When he moved over to another part of the courtyard, someone else said, "Hey, this man was with Jesus the Nazarene."

Again, Peter denied the accusation, going so far as to say, "I've never laid eyes on the man before in my life!"

Shortly after that, some other people approached him and said, "You must have come here with Jesus; your accent gives you away."

Now Peter was really scared and yelled, "I don't know who you're talking about!" Just then, a rooster crowed and Peter remembered what Jesus had told him. He had in fact denied his master three times.

Ashamed, Peter left and fell into a fit of sorrow.

REFLECTIONS

Moving into the final three chapters of the Gospel of Matthew, it quickly becomes apparent that the narrative has changed regarding the way we see Jesus. He is no longer the outspoken prophet standing before large crowds gathered to hear his message or be healed by his touch. Rather, he is shown to be a young man pensively and, at times, fearfully contemplating the end of his earthly life.

As the narrative unfolds, we are invited to witness the events leading up to Jesus' death and resurrection through the eyes of an unseen bystander. Bearing witness to the first intimate moment, we find Jesus and his disciples gathered for dinner at the house of Simon, where a woman approaches and anoints him with expensive perfume. When his disciples chastise her wasting the fragrance, we can almost feel Jesus' dismay at their reaction, for here is a stranger who is obviously more aware of the significance of what is happening than his twelve most intimate friends and students.

Around this time, the disciple Judas has slipped away in secret to ask a group of Jewish priests how much they will pay him to reveal the whereabouts of Jesus. They offer him thirty pieces of silver, and though the amount is not necessarily relevant, the transaction invites us all to consider whether there is any amount of money which would similarly entice us to betray a dear friend. In my own life, I have seen money change people who, until the opportunity was presented, would have sworn themselves incapable of such betrayal.

During Passover dinner the following evening, Jesus lets his disciples know that one of them will soon betray him, a statement that sends a wave of shock and disbelief through the room. For the past three years, these thirteen men have lived together, bounded by a mission that will end up launching one of the world's major religions. Imagine the dismay everyone (other than Judas) must have felt knowing that one of them had turned against Jesus.

Later, as he passes bread and wine around the table, we realize that Jesus is offering the first communion; an invitation for those present to consider the bread and wine as his body and blood, which will soon be sacrificed for all mankind. I have heard and read many complicated dissections of this ritual but, for me, it is a simple reminder that, in the most dire of circumstances, we should all be willing to lay down our lives for each other. Many people believe that there is a far more metaphysical meaning behind this communion, but when we look back at Jesus' ministry, we see that he has offered his disciples numerous lessons and examples for them to emulate as they go out on ministries of their own.

After dinner, they make their way to the Mount of Olives and the Garden of Gethsemane, where Jesus makes it clear that they will all soon abandon him and scatter like fearful sheep from the events about to transpire. In response, Peter, his dearest friend, says this could never happen.

This is a relatable moment, for while we all want to believe that we will remain loyal and adhere to our highest principles and convictions in the most trying of times, most of us will buckle under fear and do whatever is needed to stay alive. In fact, we only need to read the next verse to realize that, as Jesus is walking and praying in the garden, he himself is afraid of losing his life and asks God whether there is any other way to serve his purpose to humanity. But as is poignantly described in the verse, the difference between Jesus and most people is that he ultimately knows he is here to surrender to the will of his Heavenly Father rather than obey the fearful voice of self-preservation.

When he returns to his disciples, he discovers that Judas has led a group of Jewish priests and their servants to seize him and turn him over to Roman officials. During the scuffle that ensues, one of the disciples draws a sword and slices the ear of one of the servants, which prompts Jesus to utter his last words to his companions before being crucified. We can almost hear the pleading tone in his voice as he reminds them that all who live by violence are destined to die by violence, which I believe is one of the most important and concise teachings of his ministry.

After being taken away by the priests and their servants, Jesus is brought to the house of Caiaphas, where he is interrogated, mocked and beaten by the group. Finally, though he never personally states that he is the Messiah, his words come close enough to an admission that they charge him as a blasphemer, a crime punishable by death.

CHAPTER TWENTY-SEVEN

The End of Physical Life

At dawn's first light, the priests and religious leaders met to discuss and coordinate their final plans to put Jesus on trial. Once this was done, they tied him up and took him over to Pontius Pilate, the Roman Governor of Jerusalem.

Meanwhile, Judas was beginning to realize the full impact of his actions. Overcome with remorse, he approached the priests and threw the silver coins at them, proclaiming, "I have sinned and betrayed an innocent man."

The priests could not have cared less and decided to use Judas' money to buy a field as a burial place for foreigners.

This would be in accordance with the prophecy,

'They took the thirty silver pieces, the price determined by some of the sons of Israel, and they purchased the Potter's Field.'

Unwittingly, the priests who offered the thirty silver pieces and bought the land had contributed to the prophesy coming true.

Before long, Jesus was standing in front of Pontius Pilate and the gallery of priests and scholars.

Pilate began his questioning. "Are you the King of the Jews?"

Jesus was elusive. "Those are your words, not mine."

As the accusations started flying from the gallery, Jesus kept quiet.

Pilate asked him, "Do you hear all these claims they are making about you? Aren't you going to say something in your defense?" When Jesus still would not answer, Pilate found himself being impressed by Jesus' resolve in the face of mortal danger.

There was an old custom during the feast that allowed the governor to pardon a single prisoner named by the crowd. At the time, an infamous criminal named Barabbas was in prison. Since a number of people were already in attendance, Pilate asked, "Which prisoner shall I pardon? Barabbas, a known felon, or Jesus, the so-called Messiah?" Pilate was aware that it was sheer spite from the religious leaders that had brought Jesus there, and he figured the crowd might not be as vengeful.

While court was still in session, Pilate's wife sent him a message saying, "Don't get involved in the judgment of this man Jesus. I've just had a terrible night's sleep because of a dream I've had about him."

But as this was going on, the priests had rallied the crowd and talked them into pardoning Barabbas instead of Jesus.

When the time came, Pilate appeared before them and asked, "Which of these two men do you want me to pardon?"

"Barabbas!" they shouted back.

"Then what is to become of Jesus, the so-called Christ?"

"Execute him! Nail him to a cross!"

Pilate objected. "But for what crime?"

There was no reasoning with the frenzied mob. "Crucify him!"

When Pilate saw that he wasn't getting anywhere with the crowd, he walked over to a bowl of water and said, "I wash my hands of this judgment. From now on, Jesus' blood will be on your hands! You are both the judge and the jury in this case!"

"We will take the blame. We and all of our children after us!"

Then Pilate pardoned Barabbas and handed Jesus over to be whipped and crucified.

The governor's soldiers took Jesus into the palace, where they hatched a plan to further ridicule him as the "King of the Jews." They stripped him and put him in a red toga to represent a royal cloak, then fashioned a crown from thorny branches and placed it on his head. For a scepter, they put a stick in his hand. When they were done, they knelt before him in mock reverence, chanting, "All hail the mighty King of the Jews! Bravo!" Then they spit on him and beat him with the stick. Following this cruelty, they took off the toga and put his own clothes back on before proceeding with the crucifixion.

As they headed out, they came upon a man from Cyrene named Simon and made him carry the cross that Jesus would be crucified upon. When they arrived at Golgotha, which means "Skull Hill," they offered Jesus a solution of wine and myrrh as a slight painkiller, but he rejected it. Wasting no time, they nailed him to the cross and afterwards spent their time throwing dice to see who would get his clothes after he died. Above his head, they posted a sign that read, "This is Jesus, King of the Jews." Along with him, two others were being crucified that day; one to his right and one to his left.

People passing by stopped to jeer or shake their heads. They shouted out spiteful things like, "You bragged that you could tear down the temple and rebuild it in three days, so let's see it! Why, you can't even save yourself. If you're really God's son, let's see you come down from that cross!"

The high priests and scholars weren't going to miss out on the spectacle and shouted, "He saved others, did he? Well, let's see if he can save himself. King of Israel, is he? Then why doesn't he come down from that cross? Maybe then we will believe him! He was so sure God would protect him. Well, where is God now to rescue his son? That is what he claimed, right? That he was God's son?"

Even the two criminals at his sides started to mock him.

Beginning around midday, a foreboding darkness came over the land. Then, in the late afternoon, Jesus groaned and cried out, "Eli, Eli, lama sabachthani' which means, "My God, my God, why have you abandoned me?"

Some people who heard him said, "Listen, he's calling out to Elijah." One of them ran and got a sponge, soaked it in some wine and raised it on a stick so Jesus could drink. The others joked, "Don't be in such a hurry. Let's see if Elijah comes to save him."

But at that moment, Jesus, with a moan of anguish, released his last breath.

Soon afterward, strange things are reported to have happened. The darkness that had been hovering over them was suddenly torn wide open. There was a great earthquake, splitting rocks and exposing some tombs that had been dug into the hillsides. It is said that many of the people who had been buried in those tombs were later seen walking around the city.

The Roman captain and the soldiers who had witnessed these amazing events became afraid. "Surely, this was the son of God!" they exclaimed.

There were also quite a few women, many of whom had been following Jesus to serve him, who were watching from a safe distance. Among them were Mary Magdalene, Mary the mother of James and Joseph, and the mother of the Zebedee brothers.

Late in the afternoon, a wealthy man from Arimathea arrived. His name was Joseph, and since he had been a follower of Jesus, he approached Pontius Pilate to ask for Jesus' body. The governor agreed, and Joseph took the body, wrapped it in clean linens, and placed it in a newly hollowed hillside tomb which he had ordered for himself.

After Jesus was placed inside the tomb, a huge rock was rolled into place to seal the entrance. Joseph then left the site, but Mary Magdalene and the other Mary decided to stay, finding a place to sit in plain view of the tomb.

After sundown, the high priests and Pharisees arranged a meeting with Pilate, saying, "We just remembered something. When that liar Jesus was alive, he said he would rise up from the dead in three days. We need you to post a guard at his tomb so his followers don't steal the body and say, 'Look! He *was* raised from the dead!' Then we'll be worse off than before, his final deceit surpassing all the others."

Pilate agreed, saying, "I will give you some of my guards. Take them with you and secure the tomb as you see fit."

Once they received his permission, they rushed out and secured the tomb, then posted the guards outside of it for the next three days.

REFLECTIONS

The last we hear from any of Jesus' disciples in this powerful chapter is when Judas, racked with guilt for betraying his teacher and friend, returns to the Jewish priests and throws the silver coins at their feet. Then, as is told in this particular account, he goes out into a field and hangs himself. It is interesting to note that, in Luke the apostle's Book of Acts, it is reported that Judas keeps the money and uses it to buy a plot of land, which he works before accidentally falling into a ditch and dying in it. I am not sure how these two conflicting versions made it into the canonized Bible, but at least they do both agree on the essential fact that Judas is the person who betrays Jesus and, in one way or another, dies an untimely death in a parcel of land known as Potter's Field.

With Roman prefect Pontius Pilate presiding, the trial and sentencing leading up to Jesus' crucifixion happens quickly. Pilate, most likely not accustomed to Jewish law, begins his interrogation by asking Jesus outright whether he is the self-proclaimed King of the Jews.

At this point, it does not seem to matter much as to how Jesus answers, for his accusers have already deemed him guilty of the crime of blasphemy. And of course, by not directly denying the charge, he gives the priests all the ammunition they need to proceed with their allegations.

In physics, the word *trajectory* is used to explain the arc of a physical projectile through space. This is useful in the pursuit of projecting where a launched missile will land or tracing the path of a planet as it orbits the sun. But there are also trajectories to life, and at this juncture in the story, Jesus is fully aware of the events which must take place for his ministry to have its intended impact. He knows that, while his life could have had many other outcomes, only the one where he is executed will serve the true meaning and purpose of his existence. As such, the trajectory of Jesus' life is so firmly set that not even a Roman prefect can stand in the way of its course.

In Jesus' final moments of his earthly existence, he continues to be mocked by the crowd, who are now gathered beneath him as he hangs on the cross. When he finally releases his last anguished breath, he pleads, "Father, father, why have you abandoned me?" There are other accounts of what he says as his final words, most famously, "It is finished" or "Forgive them Father, for they know not what they do," which you may read about in the gospels of John and Luke. Regardless, it is clear that, while Jesus did indeed express fear and doubt about his death, he willingly relinquished his life to God and died with his beliefs and principles intact. He made no plea for vengeance, he did not incite people to riot or protest; he died a gruesome and humiliating death in front of the people he was trying to save.

We sometimes hear about military personnel or police officers who have "made the ultimate sacrifice" by dying in the line of duty, but we often ignore the fact that part of their duty is being trained, armed and prepared to kill. And while these brave men and women can certainly be considered heroes, there is a big difference between their sacrifice and the one made by Jesus. He died adhering to his beliefs in non-violence so that others—regardless of their beliefs—may live.

CHAPTER TWENTY-EIGHT

The Dawn of a New Era

At the end of the Sabbath, in the early light of dawn on Sunday, Mary Magdalene and the other Mary came to keep watch at the tomb. Suddenly, the earth quaked and rocked, and the stone seal on the tomb rolled to the side as an angel appeared before them. The angel's appearance was bright like lightning, and the Roman guards stationed there were frozen with fear at the sight of this radiant being.

Before long, the angelic visitor spoke to the women, saying, "Don't be afraid. I know you are looking for Jesus, the one they nailed to a cross, but he isn't here. Just as he told you, death had no claim on him. Come and look for yourselves at the empty tomb!"

In a state of shock and disbelief, the women did as they were told and could barely believe that Jesus' body was nowhere to be found.

The angel left them with these words, "Now, hurry back to the disciples and tell them what you have seen here today. Also, let them know that Jesus will be waiting for them in Galilee."

The women, overcome with elation, wasted no time in leaving the tomb. On their way back to break the amazing news to the disciples, Jesus himself appeared to them. "Good morning," he said and they fell to their knees, kissing his feet in worship. "Blessed sisters, you are holding onto me for dear life! Don't be afraid, and please pass this message on to my brothers, 'Go to Galilee, and I will meet you there.'"

Meanwhile, a few of the frightened guards had run back into the city, where they told the high priests everything they had witnessed. Soon after, an emergency meeting was called, and the religious leaders quickly put a plan into action. They decided to bribe the Roman guards into saying that they had fallen asleep and that Jesus' disciples had stolen the body in the night. The leaders also offered the guards assurance that they would receive no punishment. The soldiers took the bribe and stuck to the story cooked up by the Jewish High Council, which has been circulating ever since.

As they had been instructed, the eleven remaining disciples made their way to Galilee to see if the women's story was true. The moment they saw Jesus, they were struck with awe and worshipped him. Even so, a few of them found it hard to believe that he really had risen from the dead.

While he could understand how difficult this was for them to accept, Jesus was not deterred from the purpose of their gathering. Making sure he had their full attention, he delivered his commission.

"God has authorized and commanded me to give you an assignment. Go out and tell everyone you meet that the way I have lived my life and the things I have taught are indeed the way to salvation. It does not matter where they come from or what religion they may adhere to; let them all know that they have a Loving Creator and that they are all His beloved children. Tell them that they share an eternal bond with God, a bond that began long before they arrived here on Earth and will continue afterward in the eternal Kingdom of Heaven. Model for them the ways of love, compassion, and forgiveness, for this is the true path to humanity's redemption. And should you falter along your journey, take heart, because I will always be connected to you— eternal spirit to eternal spirit—until the end of this age."

Reflections

This final, powerful chapter picks up the story with Mary Magdalene and Mary of Jacob returning to the tomb on the third day following Jesus' crucifixion. One can only imagine the range of emotions they must have felt—from shock, to fear, to elation—as Jesus appears and instructs them to direct his disciples to Galilee.

I find it interesting that, while his disciples are conspicuously absent during the entire ordeal of his trial, crucifixion, burial, and resurrection, these two brave women are the first witnesses to the most significant event in the entire story, Jesus' resurrection.

Many scholars believe that Mary Magdalene was not only a constant companion during his ministry, but also a direct influence on his teachings. Keep in mind that, in the culture of Jesus' day, women were often regarded as second-class citizens, so the significant role these women played during the birth of Christianity cannot be overstated.

As had been arranged, Jesus meets his disciples in Galilee, where they are all obviously astounded to see him. In the Gospel of John, Thomas is described as being the most dubious of this miracle, and Jesus addresses Thomas' doubts by allowing him to insert a finger into an open wound inflicted by a Roman soldier.

To this day, we often refer to an incredulous person as being a "Doubting Thomas," a direct reference to this interaction.

I love that the instructions Jesus gives his disciples in this meeting are so brief and concise. While these men must be more confused than ever and surely have many questions, their inquiries are preempted by a short yet powerful commission. They are told to spread out and share the good news of God's love for everyone—no matter where they are from or what they believe—for all time. In the simplest way possible, Jesus reminds them that salvation will come to all who emulate the way he lived on Earth.

While many people have doubts regarding who and what Jesus was or is, few can argue that what he commanded us all to do—love, respect and forgive each other without limit—represents the only path that will save our species. This is by no means an easy order to follow, but it *is* a simple one. So simple, in fact, that even a child can grasp it. And isn't that what he told us all along? Unless we are as innocent and pure as children, the Kingdom of Heaven will remain forever elusive.

As both John the Baptist and Jesus proclaimed, the Kingdom of Heaven is not only residing within each and every one of us, it is waiting to be expressed *through* us in every moment. It is time for us to recognize that we are all children of God, and there could be no more urgent time to recognize this fact than right now. We are not lowly sinners fumbling blindly in the dark, we are each divinity in human form remembering our way home to Heaven.

But time is of the essence. Humanity's old ways of employing destruction and death to resolve our differences must come to an end if we are to ascend into Christ Consciousness. Jesus proved this is possible while here on Earth, and all he ever asked of any of us was to follow his example. He did not say we had to worship him, or slay an enemy of non-believers, or even attend church.

He said we have to love one another. He implored us to *be* love, because he knew that this was the purest expression of what

God is in every dimension, which includes not only the realms of faith and belief, but also of pragmatism and science. Every new discovery made in quantum physics seems to tease out another aspect of the mysterious intelligence running behind all things, and this intelligence is making itself more known every day. As we move farther along our heroic story of understanding who we are, how we came to be, and the purpose of our existence, we are realizing that we are not mistakes or the result of random genetic mutations. We are not earthly beings having momentary spiritual experiences, we are spiritual beings having a momentary earthly experience. We are the means by which Source is recognizing and experiencing itself through everything we think, say, and do.

The journey of awakening begins with each new moment, and Jesus' words live on to advise and comfort us every step of the way.

What Should We Believe?

Throughout the last 2,000 years, people familiar with the story of Jesus have come to some personal conclusions about who he was and what he means to us today.

For devout Christians, he was the most unique being who has ever existed on this planet—a fully human man who was also fully God. To these believers, every biblical reference to Jesus and the miraculous nature of his life is to be taken literally and as absolute fact.

To many spiritual seekers, Jesus stands shoulder-to-shoulder with other historical prophets and philosophers who dedicated their lives to expanding human consciousness. In this view, Jesus was a spiritual master who may even have been capable of performing some of the miracles mentioned in the Gospels.

Still others hold the opinion that, while Jesus might have been a great spiritual teacher, his supernatural abilities were exaggerated through stories passed along in the oral tradition before anything was ever written about him.

Some say the man named Jesus as described in the Bible never existed at all.

At different times in my life, I have found myself either accepting or doubting each of these beliefs to some degree. Was he really born from a virgin? And what about raising the dead, turning water into wine, or transmuting himself into a being of pure light? While I have often felt that I must suspend critical thinking to accept these accounts, I eventually came to realize that what often separates "reality" from a miracle is simply the passage of time. Imagine telling someone 150 years ago that humans would soon be flying across the sky, or walking on the moon... they would hardly even be able to comprehend what you were talking about. As Novelist Arthur C. Clarke famously quoted, "Magic is just science we don't understand yet."

Even Einstein came to a certain peace with the incredible nature of our existence when he realized that there are two ways to think about our lives—one in which nothing is a miracle, the other where *everything* is a miracle.

Consider the complex yet elegant design of our DNA. We have learned much about its structure and composition over the past few decades, but there is far more that we do not know. To that point, over 90% of our genetic coding serves no known function, and so is often referred to as "junk DNA." But what if this currently dormant part of our genetic makeup is what will make future miracles possible? In the quantum realm of an entangled universe, it is not absurd to imagine things like extra-sensory perception, telekinesis, energy healing or even levitation once the entire spectrum of our DNA is fully activated. Did Jesus have premature access to this information, thus making him able to calm stormy waters or heal others through a simple touch? We may never know, but in the quantum universe these occurrences are not beyond the realm of possibility.

And though my perception of miracles has broadened over the years, there have been other issues of doubt I've had to address. For instance, to my analytical mind, if Jesus did indeed make the profound impact the Gospels tell us he had on people, there should be other forms of corroborative proof of his existence. Unfortunately, there is very little tangible evidence to validate the biblical accounts of Jesus' life and ministry. Only in the last few decades have historians discovered brief mentions by both Roman and Jewish scribes stating that a man named Yeshua, who had a brother named James, was sentenced to death by Roman Prefect Pontius Pilate. For spiritual skeptics like me, it is comforting to think that the Gospels are based on some degree of truth, and that it is possible that the words attributed to Jesus were actually spoken by him.

For those who have come to the conclusion that Jesus did exist but was not the miracle worker or savior as described in the Bible, the absence of historical evidence can easily bolster your doubts. But lack of evidence is not the same as evidence, and while I have at times lived in this place of uncertainty, I have also come to realize that accepting the potential of truth is the first step to arriving at truth. For instance, the earliest scientists suspected there could be a relationship between gravity and velocity long before there was ever any proof of this correlation.

I hope this book has helped you in some way. Writing it has been a cathartic exercise for me, bringing a certain peace surrounding a man named Jesus, who eventually became known as *Christ*, or, in ancient Greek, "the anointed one." And while I still have questions, I'm much more comfortable with the idea that Jesus was something more than the sum of the oral stories, anecdotes, hymns, political agendas and even wars fought in his name.

In the early 18th century, the French philosopher Voltaire said, "If God did not exist, it would be necessary to invent Him." This was not to be taken as a blasphemous or inflammatory statement, rather one that points to the human condition of yearning to know and understand the architect of our lives. In the same way Voltaire considered God, humanity *needs* a figure like Jesus—a guide who is not only pointing the way to our eternal heavenly home, but who has also told and shown us how to get there. It is no surprise to me that Jesus' teachings of unconditional love, compassion and forgiveness resonate more strongly now than ever, his ministry serving as a beautiful testament to the highest potential of our species.

As I navigate the peaks and valleys ahead on my spiritual path, I will continue to read the gospels—and also the teachings of prophets and sages like Buddha, Krishna, Lao Tzu and Mohammed. We are all learning at our own pace and experiencing life in our way, each tasked with keeping our hearts and minds open enough to honor each other's journey of awakening.

With words that stand the test of time, Jesus urged us to always shine our light, treat others with the same respect in which we wish to be treated, and never forget that the Kingdom of Heaven is already residing within each and every one of us.

Printed in Dunstable, United Kingdom

65649387R00109